THE JOURNEY: A GUIDE FOR PERSONS, PARTNERS, AND PARENTS

Doug Meske, MSW, Ph.D.
Kathie Amidei, MA, Ed.D.

ISBN 978-0-615-76472-6

Printed by R & R Communication
Waukesha, WI

Edited by Lea Boyd

Foreword

Throughout the years in school we study numerous subjects. The courses taken help us learn the meaning of the past, contribute to an understanding of the world in the present and try to prepare us for the future. So much of our education and preparation for life focuses on our life experiences and the world outside of us. It is quite obvious how important it is to become adequate and actually skilled at dealing with the world. We need to make decisions about how to make a living, find a career that fits, where to live, and who we might want to live with. Just think about the long list of realistic tasks that will come with the concept of dealing with life in day to day living!

However, in order to be really effective and find satisfaction with daily life and to have inner peace, it is also essential to be effective with the most important relationship in our life, the relationship with our self and our own inner peace. Throughout one's life, we will have both personal and interpersonal tasks that need attention. This book is to serve as a guide, a map, to help on that journey through life. We travel this journey living various roles, as a person, perhaps as a partner, and perhaps as a parent. We refer to this as the "Journey of Persons, Partners and Parents". Individually and together, we are on, as the song says, the "Circle of Life". The circle is an appropriate metaphor. Life goes around from one role to another, from challenge and joy, to success and goodness, from beginning to end, without knowing when the end will happen. For even though our journeys are individual, the circle points to the connectedness we all share, in personal relationships, in being part of local communities and in fact, as we learn more and more each day, as part of the global community. We are truly challenged on this journey to know and care for ourselves, to relate effectively with others, and to be responsible in the growth and development of others.

Just as a dashboard on a car tells us what is going on inside the car, (when we need gas or oil, what the temperature is, how fast we are going, how many miles we have traveled), so too our emotions tell us what is going on inside of us. Just as we wouldn't drive a car with the dashboard covered up, we shouldn't go through life not being aware of our emotions and emotional needs. Life is richer and we are more effective when we:

1. get to know what our emotional needs are
2. learn how to take care of them
3. discover how to get along and to live with others

These are critical tasks for our overall well-being and stability. For persons of faith, closely related, is the importance of becoming aware of our spiritual hungers. Like our emotional needs, spiritual hungers may also not be noticed because they are invisible. But they, too, are part of our humanity and need our attention. Our spiritual hungers, attended to, can lead to greater satisfaction and happiness on our life journey as well as to help us keep an eye to the ultimate reality and the eternal reality even as we are fully present to life here and now.

It is from our experience of working for many years with individuals and families that we offer this "inner roadmap". It is our belief that a culture that calls so much of our attention to the world outside of our emotions and spirit can cause us to neglect our heart and soul. Our hope is that this book is encouragement to pay attention to the emotional needs and spiritual hungers that create the rich fabric for a full life. Most of us know when we are living in the fullness of life versus when we are not, and we feel a sense of "something missing." Our hope is that by reading, thinking, discussing, and working on what we share in this book, it will serve as a guide, as direction to making your journey fulfilling, healthy, and more joyful.

This book is written in an informal style because we hope it is read on a very personal level. If we could, we would like to be sitting across from each person reading this and having a personal conversation. Our hope is that spending time with this book will help you with these goals:

1. To move toward an understanding of all that you are and all that you can be.
2. To arrange your priorities and direct your energies so that you can take care of what really needs to be seen as crucial

and learn what you must do for yourself and with others to be healthy, effective and generally happy.

3. To recognize and appreciate the role of other people in your life and how important you are in theirs.
4. To realize how similar we all are. We are sisters and brothers. We really do need one another. We are family.
5. And, maybe, if we open our hearts and minds and trust to imagine, we can catch a glimpse of the bigger picture. Each of us has been created with a wonderful body, mind, and spirit that gathers all the gifts of being human and touches them with the love of God that created us and binds us all together. That dimension of us, once understood, is eternal and can be blessing us in this life and beyond.

In his book, *The Road Less Traveled,* Scott Peck begins with the sentence, "Life is difficult." As we all know, life can certainly be difficult. It can be many things. It can be happy or sad, clear or confusing, peaceful or upsetting, difficult or easy, comfortable or anxious, rewarding or disappointing, consistent or unpredictable, fulfilling or empty, resolved or unfinished, exciting or flat. Yes, life certainly can be a journey, an experience with numerous moments when we feel one way or another.

Although there are times in life when we have little or no control over what happens, there are many more times when what happens and how we end up feeling are up to us. We determine these times and moments. We are the captains of our destiny and how life goes; but be careful – we're not saying all the time. We understand that things like illness, unemployment, the weather, the economy, and the decisions someone else makes are beyond our control. It's times like these when we are not in control, that the best we can do is learn to cope effectively with what we can't change and to trust in God's care.

However, aside from these times in our lives, the point is that, much more of the time than not, we determine our lives. Personally, and in our interpersonal relationships with others, we must hold ourselves and others accountable for how life goes. We must take responsibility for how we end up feeling about our lives. We must take responsibility for initiating what will happen or not happen in our relationships with others. The bottom line? We need to see ourselves and the significant others in our lives as the designers of the journey.

The purpose of this book is to assist you in designing your journey and to learn to travel effectively as a person, as a partner, and as a parent. This book will address:

- the importance of knowing and caring for six specific emotional needs in your life.
- how to make sure your marriage is a healthy, rewarding, successful relationship.
- what to do to build a healthy family in a society that is not very healthy.
- the do's and don'ts for couples going through divorce and how to protect your children.
- ways to strengthen your spirituality, your prayer life, and your relationship with God.

Before we start working together on the journey, let us tell you a little bit about ourselves. We want you to understand why we think we have something valuable to offer you and your loved ones.

From our own personal lives and because of the people we have been blessed to work with and we have many ideas we want to share with you. We offer you the "inner roadmap" to journey personally and in your relationships with your spouse and children. It is our belief and our concern that our current society puts so much unhealthy attention to the world around us. This unhealthy focus can lead us to neglect our hearts, minds, and souls. Our hope is that this book will be encouragement and solid direction to help you pay attention to the emotional needs and spiritual hungers that create the rich fabric for a full life.

We are a therapist (Doug) and a religious educator and pastoral associate (Kathie). Doug has written from the emotional perspective and Kathie from the spiritual perspective. We both are spouses, parents, and grandparents in our respective families. We are fellow travelers on this circle of life. It is our hope that from the years we have been learning, from both our professional and personal lives, we can effectively share with you what we have learned. By doing so, we hope that the inner journey of your life will be as Jesus suggested- “life in abundance.”

Dr. Doug Meske & Dr. Kathie Amidei

About the Authors

Dr. Doug Meske has been in practice offering individual, couple and family therapies since 1968. He has been a national lecturer since 1985. He has a BA from St. Francis Seminary, M.S.W. from the University of Wisconsin-Milwaukee, an Ed.M. from Loyola of Chicago and a Ph.D. from Marquette and Clayton Universities. Clinical Memberships have included National Association of Social Workers, American Association of Christian Counselors and American Academy of Psychotherapies. He is married to Rosie, has three sons, four grandchildren and lives in Oconomowoc Wisconsin.

Dr. Kathie Amidei is a Pastoral Associate at St. Anthony on the Lake Parish in Pewaukee, Wisconsin. She is a national speaker for Our Sunday Visitor Catholic Publisher. She was formerly the Associate Director for Child Ministry for the Archdiocese of Milwaukee, a Catholic schoolteacher and director of religious education. She holds a BS in education from the University of Wisconsin-Milwaukee and an MA in theology from Sacred Heart Seminary and an Ed. D. in Leadership from Cardinal Stritch University. Kathie is married to Jim. She is the mother of adult children and a grandmother.

How to Use this Book

The overall format of this book is to discuss the Six Emotional Needs and the Five Spiritual Hungers, as they relate to the emotional and spiritual health of individuals, couples, and families, with a chance to reflect on each aspect. There are personal reflection exercises included at the end of each section. Some people find it effective to pause and reflect on what they read. You might find a blank journal or notebook especially helpful for this. Feel free to take notes when you read a key point that resonates with you. Maybe even copy a phrase from the book that you wish to remember and apply to your daily life. Make a note of what page it was from, in case you want to go back and reread that part in the book.

When you come to the reflective exercises, go ahead and write down your answers in your journal. You may find that writing your thoughts helps. Sometimes writing can also help you process what you're thinking and maybe even come to new insights or perspectives. You might consider dating each entry and skipping a few lines when you finish each entry, to allow you to come back and add in additional thoughts upon rethinking an idea or after you try out an activity. Let the journal be a tool to help you remember important information from the text and mark your thoughts as you make this journey. It is our desire that you make this book your own, a tool to bring the elements of your personal and interpersonal journey into focus and perspective in a way that makes your journey richer and more precious.

Chapter Outlines

Self-Assessment Exercise

To begin, let's take some time on a personal inventory, a personal assessment. Just like we would become physically ill if we didn't eat properly or get enough sleep, so too we will become emotionally ill if we don't take care of our emotional needs. Do you have some personal work to do for yourself because of what did or did not happen in your life from birth to age 14, from 14 – 18, from 18 to now? How would you answer the following questions?

1. I seldom worry about "what next."
2. My life and my life with others have a great deal of predictability.
3. Way too often in my life I feel nervous and on eggshells.
4. The most significant people in my life are very sensitive to the importance of voice tone.
5. I like myself.
6. I lack self-confidence.
7. Too often I think negatively about myself.
8. At the end of the day or week, I usually feel a wonderful sense of accomplishment.
9. The significant people in my life encourage me and support me in what I need to do.
10. I feel valued by others.
11. I have enough people I can count on.
12. I know I am very important to the people I want to be important to.
13. I think too much about things in my past.
14. I feel guilty too often.
15. I feel angry about former events too often.
16. I too often feel hurt about past statements made to me.
17. I am comfortable with how I can focus on the present and the future.
18. I have enough fun.

19. My significant other(s) and I have enough fun times.
20. I have no trouble "letting go" and playing.
21. I have things to look forward to every week.

Using a rating scale from 0 – 10 (10 being perfect), how would you score yourself in terms of the following statements?

1. When it comes to my moods and emotions, I am a fairly consistent and predictable person.
2. People who know me would say that I am a predictable, consistent and comfortable person to be around.
3. I sense a great deal of consistency, predictability, and trust in my life and with the people in my life.
4. Because of what I do with my life, I experience a sense of meaning, purpose, and accomplishment.
5. I have a comfortable sense of who I am.
6. I have a comfortable sense of where I am and where I'm going.
7. I think I have positive self-esteem. I think well of myself and feel confident.
8. I basically like who I am; I am pleased with myself.
9. I have good relationships with my family.
10. I have good friendships.
11. People seem to like me.
12. People seem to respect me.
13. For the most part, I am comfortable with the relationships I have in my life.
14. I am not struggling with guilt.
15. I am not handicapped to live in the present because of my past.
16. I have no major unfinished business with anyone.
17. If healthy maturity means being able to function appropriately at this time in my life, in the roles I have, I am doing quite well.
18. I have no repetitive thoughts that get in my way of enjoying life most of the time.

19. I have no repetitive feelings that get in my way of enjoying life most of the time.
20. I have activities in my life that I have fun doing.
21. I am able to play, to laugh, to enjoy myself.
22. I am able to play, to laugh, to enjoy myself without needing drugs or alcohol.
23. I have things I look forward to, both short term and long term.
24. I have a realistic attitude about life.
25. I have a fairly positive attitude about life.
26. I am clear about what's really important in life.
27. My priorities are solid and respectful.
28. I have clear and healthy values and morals.
29. I live up to my values and morals.
30. The judgments and choices I make are good for me and keep my life healthy and peaceful.
31. I have solid self-control and self-discipline.
32. When appropriate, I am able to act differently than I feel.
33. When things about me and about my life need to be changed and could be changed, I work to bring about these changes.
34. When things can't be changed, when I must have healthy coping skills to live with what can't be changed, I do a good job.
35. Consequently, I can honestly say that I work to change what should be and can be, and I cope effectively with what can't be changed.
36. I have adequate social skills.
37. I communicate effectively.
38. I listen effectively so that I understand others.
39. I don't abuse or misuse drugs or alcohol.
40. I have healthy eating habits.
41. I take good care of my physical well-being.
42. I effectively handle times when things don't go my way.
43. I am capable of compromising, of doing things the way someone else wants them done.

44. I do not compromise myself; I don't back down when what someone else wants me to do wouldn't be good for me.
45. I am strong regarding my values and priorities.
46. My anger and temper are well managed and controlled.
47. I have no addictions that influence and affect my life in unhealthy ways.
48. I behave sexually appropriately.
49. I am comfortable with my sexual identity and orientation.
50. I think I have a healthy attitude about sexual intimacy.
51. I do a good job sharing and expressing my emotions.
52. I see myself as someone who is capable of emotional intimacy – getting emotionally close to others and letting others get emotionally close to me. I let myself get involved with people, sharing my emotions and becoming somewhat vulnerable.
53. I am sensitive to the thoughts and feelings of others.

Now, having done these personal and interpersonal assessments, what would you say about yourself?

A. Do you generally feel secure and does your life have a sense of predictability and consistency?
B. At the end of a day or week, do you have a sense of accomplishment, purpose, and meaning?
C. Are you happy and confident with yourself? Do you think well of yourself and feel pleased with who you are and how you live?
D. Do you have enough relationships with whom you are comfortable? Are you confident that these people are comfortable with you? Do you have enough people with whom you feel close and special?
E. Are you at peace with your personal history, no regrets or guilts or frustrations that bother you? Are you at peace with others from your past?
F. Do you have enough fun in your life? Do you relax and play enough? Do you have enough to look forward to in life, that you happily anticipate in the future?

The chapter on Six Emotional Needs is designed to help you say "yes" to these questions. If you were able to say yes to questions A through F, then you are doing a wonderful job taking care of yourself. Keep doing whatever you are doing. If you weren't able to say "yes," then it's time you do some crucially important work for yourself. This material is going to help you with this work.

Chapter One

SIX EMOTIONAL NEEDS

I. Sense of Security
II. Sense of Accomplishment
III. Self-Esteem
IV. The Need for Relationships
V. Unfinished Business
VI. Fun and Anticipation

Six Emotional Needs

In his book, *Home Coming*, John Bradshaw affords the reader a tremendous opportunity to evaluate the effects one's childhood has had on them, and to determine what one must do to heal the child within and move on successfully in life. I have recommended this book to many people, but only with the condition that they are in therapy or have some support system to process this material. For many, *Home Coming*, or any exploration into one's history of development, proves quite difficult and potentially painful. The difficulty and degree of painfulness or joyfulness certainly vary tremendously for each of us. Each of us has our memory albums from which we can take joy or sorrow. To whatever degree you find joy, relish and savor it – because it is from this that you build your strengths and health. To whatever degree there is sorrow, recognize it and be honest about it – because it is from this that you must work to free yourself so that is doesn't continue to define you and your future. If done well, even the sorrows could eventually result in personal strength.

Scott Peck begins his book, *The Road Less Traveled*, with the sentence "Life is difficult." Each of us knows there have been times in our life when this has been true. One of our goals in life is to try to make these difficult times as few as possible, and when we cannot totally eliminate the difficult times, to then deal with them as best we can.

The first section of this book is focused on a foundation issue upon which all of our lives are dependent – *Our Six Emotional Needs*. My book with this title was first published in 1988. If you have never read this book, this first section will be very valuable to you. If you have read my first book, use this time as an opportunity to do an important review. This subject matter is presented more in depth in this book; and I am sure you can benefit a great deal from going through it again. Effectively taking care of your six emotional needs is as essential to your emotional and mental well-being as water, food, and air are to your physical well-being.

We all have basic emotional needs, which must be met in order for us to lead satisfying lives and develop healthy relationships.

David Viscott, author of *How to Live With Another Person*, emphasizes that "other people can play an important part in helping us meet these needs; however, no relationship can provide everything we need. Much of what we need must come from ourselves. Sometimes the problems we encounter in our lives become even more insurmountable because we look in the wrong places for the answers." Think of the many places we look to find meaning in our lives: food, alcohol, sexuality, spending, work, excessive volunteering, demands on others, etc. Pause here and think about where you spend a great deal of time and energy that leaves you feeling unfulfilled, frustrated, drained, and maybe even stuck in some serious trouble and pain.

Too often we focus on outlets to try to meet our emotional needs rather than discovering the appropriate, healthy ways to take care of them. It is very easy to become addicted to someone or something if it seems to temporarily answer our needs. Although these addictions may provide temporary satisfaction, in the long run these answers fall short, leaving us empty, lonely, angry, in trouble, unhealthy, and confused. We must learn to tell the difference between those people, places, and things that are truly valuable and good for us and those that are superficial, temporary, and ultimately unhealthy. We must learn to tell the difference between what "we can reasonably expect from other people – particularly from the significant people in our lives – and what we must provide for ourselves." *(Viscott)*

When I ask a group of people what their basic needs are, the answers vary – sleep, money, family, friends, water, God, love, quiet, food, air. Once someone said "perfume," and everyone in the group laughed. Yet this may be a very real need for that person. Have you ever gone back into the house to put on your perfume or cologne? Have you ever stopped at a drug store just to buy a bottle of perfume or cologne on your way to work? Probably each one of us can think of things in our lives upon which we have become dependent. I am sure we all spend an inordinate amount of time, energy, and money on "necessities", which we really could live without. Periodically we need to assess our needs and see how they are being met. Then we should refocus our priorities and define the places in our lives where we can make some changes. We must consider where our energy is directed and decide if this is the right direction. If we do not have our priorities straight and do not use our energies to care for our critical emotional needs, we will experience all sorts of negative consequences, clinically called *symptoms*.

The Painful Symptoms

Depression

One of the most common signs of being personally in trouble is depression. We all have moments when we feel sad, but sadness is not the same as depression. Sadness is a normal human feeling. It is normal and it can be crummy, but it is a healthy emotional expression of loss or disappointment. However, it is very different from depression. A good, non-clinical definition of depression would be:

1. A sadness that lasts too long.
2. A sadness that happens too often.
3. A sadness that affects much of your life.

This sadness has now grown into depression. Pharmaceutical companies have become very wealthy selling medications which decrease depression, but these medications only help the immediate feelings. They do not necessarily solve the problems caused by depression. In many cases, medication, along with good therapy, is the appropriate combination of treatments to deal effectively with depression. With depression, people need to look at themselves and to evaluate what they need to do to deal more effectively with life so that depression is not a consequence. What strategies do you have that help you change how your life is going and how you feel about it? People are accountable for their own destiny and responsible for dealing effectively with their own lives. This is where it becomes critical to know our emotional needs and to be effectively getting them cared for.

Medications

It is sad that we have somehow been conditioned to think so negatively about ourselves and to be embarrassed when we think of taking medications for psychological struggles and problems. Think of the many medical reasons people will take medications, from allergies to vitamins, headaches, arthritis, and many serious illnesses. In all these cases, people are thankful for the scientific discovery and seem to have no embarrassment for the medicational need. However, mention medications for mood and behavioral problems, and people have tremendous struggles.

For sure when the problem is within the chemical imbalance of the person, medications are a necessity. It makes no more sense to try to deal with depression or anxieties that are physically based without medications than it would be to deal with allergies or diabetes without medications. The person has no power over these. The depression is a condition and a consequence of their physiologic system.

Sometimes people are so fragile with fears, hurts, angers, or feeling overwhelmed that for a while a "crutch" is necessary until their strength returns enough to function without the crutch. The crutch in the case of depression is the medication. It serves to aid the healing process. It serves to support and to carry the person for a while until his or her own strength and capabilities are developed to deal with life without the medication. Medications should be seen and appreciated as an aid to getting well. This is how people should try to understand and to appreciate medications. When struggling with depression, especially severe depression, people should regard medications as a wonderful helping agent as they work on themselves in therapy.

Frustration

Another symptom of being emotionally unhealthy is frustration. Do you often say to yourself, "Oh, I'll tolerate that," or "I'm not going to make a big deal of that," or "I don't want to talk about that," or "I'm not going to rock the boat?" In all of these examples, someone or something is upsetting you, but you apparently do not see any value in speaking up or you believe that speaking of it will only make the situation worse. Doubting that change is possible leads to thoughts of hopelessness, and hopelessness leads to depression and discouragement. Life without hope, without believing in the potential for change and improvement is depressing, discouraging, and frustrating. "He or she will not change." "Things will never be any different around here." "What difference does it make what I do, it won't matter."

Such negative thinking can lead to a kind of frustrated depression we talked about previously or to a frustrated anger and even explosiveness. Notice what we're doing here… we are identifying a number of symptoms or "warning signs":

- Frustration leading to hopelessness, leading to depression
- Frustration leading to irritability, walking on eggshells, being anxious
- Frustration leading to anger
- Frustration leading to rage

What is the common denominator? What is this frustration all about? Wouldn't a good definition for this frustration be "a feeling we experience when someone or something is not living up to what we expected or what we believed should happen, and it won't change?" We experience frustration when we think we can't talk about it or can't do anything to change a situation. The common denominator is that expectations have not been lived up to. What we counted on, hoped for, or believed in, will not happen. We are certainly disappointed, and disappointment can certainly result in sadness. It's very important to pay attention to when the disappointments are causing you inner tension and upset. This is frustration. Frustration can result in depression or different levels of agitation, upset, and anxiety.

Plus, this frustration gets exacerbated when we are trying to tolerate some expectation that's going unmet and, in reality, it is not tolerable. We are trying to tolerate what is not tolerable. In trying to do so, we will have personal or interpersonal consequences. Imagine how long you could tolerate not eating, drinking, sleeping or breathing. What's your tolerance level? Have you tried to tolerate not breathing for minutes? Have you tried to tolerate what isn't tolerable, in life, in relationships? What will happen? Keep this concept in mind throughout your reading about the emotional needs.

When you look at your list of people or places in your life that cause you frustration, is the common denominator that your expectations are not being lived up to? Does it seem that how you expected someone to behave or how you expected something to be done just didn't go as you anticipated? So often, this results in frustration.

What are you doing to prevent frustration? Who in your life needs to do a better job at living up to your appropriate expectations? Where in your life, or with whom should you expect less? Commit to some good homework in this area.

As we go through the various symptoms that tell us something is wrong, that some emotional need is going unmet, watch how the concept of expectations keeps coming up. This is a very important concept, one we will touch on throughout this book. For now the emphasis is on the fact that if you are trying to tolerate what is not tolerable, you are developing a tremendous frustration that can result in emotional and/or physical problems.

Irritability

A related symptom to frustration as a warning sign is excessive irritability. Becoming upset over something that in reality does not deserve such a reaction is a sign of excessive irritability. Do you suddenly become angry or feel touchy about little things? One night I came home, took off my tie and got upset at my 8-year-old son for wrinkling the tie when he was actually trying to help me by folding it up and putting it away. Obviously, I was feeling pressure that had nothing to do with the tie or my son. The tie wasn't the issue. My son didn't deserve the reaction. The reaction itself was ridiculous. Do you ever find yourself in the middle of a heated argument and suddenly forget what you were arguing about? Or, do you think, "What we were arguing about was so silly and insignificant." These are signs that the stress factors in your life are increasing and that something below the surface is going on. The sense of being on-edge and touchy is a warning sign. Pay attention to it; understand it; discover what it's really about.

Extreme Anger / Overreaction

Extreme anger or overreaction is a serious symptom. If you find yourself blowing your stack because the grocery store clerk has to check the price of bananas, because your spouse is nine minutes late, or because your child spilled his milk, then you need to ask yourself, "Why am I letting something this small get so out of proportion?" Children and spouses tend to be the most frequent victims of our overreactions. We no longer "kick the cat." Instead, we lash out at the ones we love. Excessive irritability, extreme anger, overreaction… I see so much of these in my practice; let's spend some time looking at them. Do any of the following sound familiar to you?

- Negative tone of voice
- Volume, too loud
- The look on your face
- Body language that conveys being upset
- Vulgarity
- Explosive behavior (yelling, throwing things, breaking things, physically striking out)
- Becoming teary too quickly
- Blaming
- Being overly sensitive, overly devastated, crushed
- Saying things you later regret

Recognizing these in yourself and listening to others who point these out to you are ways to begin changing them. However, the real change lies in discovering what is really missing or going on in your life that is causing these behaviors. To take care of the headache with aspirin is not sufficient if the real problem is a pinched nerve in your neck.

Emptiness

A frequent feeling of emptiness is another symptom of being emotionally unhealthy. Do you think you do not have anything to look forward to, that life is just drudgery, or that a sense of meaning is absent? This joyless approach to life is a serious problem. Surely we all have some moments, perhaps even a few days, like this. But this feeling should not become a constant companion. There are a number of ways you can offset this emptiness. You have heard people refer to their "fun meter." On a scale of 1 to 10 what does your meter read? You may want to do a fun meter inventory for the different roles, times, and places in your life. Make a list of your various roles, activities, responsibilities, and relationships and check out how enjoyable these roles are for you. If your list hits 20 roles or more, this is not uncommon. Be thorough. Think of all the roles you have that result in various activities, some with various people. Do you find these times enjoyable? Do you look forward to them? What do your answers tell you?

Now let's be careful. Fun should not be your only scale. Often the feeling of emptiness can be improved through a sense of meaning or purpose or by having enjoyable relationships. Any given activity or role might not be particularly fun, but you gain a sense of fulfillment from doing it or from being in that role. You know what you just did was worthwhile, even if you had to push yourself to do it. There's a sense of value and appreciation that comes from what you did, either from within yourself or from others. Where in your life do you have this? Take some time to reflect on this. Ask yourself if there are some changes needing to be made so that you feel more fulfilled and purposeful. Where? Doing what? For whom? With whom? We'll talk more about preventing or lessening emptiness as we get into the emotional needs.

Sexual Difficulties

Sexual difficulties are frequently signals that something is bothering you, either in your own life or in your relationship with someone else. These difficulties may take the form of lack of desire, lack of excitement, or lack of specific sexual responses. Lack of desire occurs when you have lengths of time without sexual interest. No one can establish a time frame for someone else. You are your own judge. You will know, if you are honest with yourself, when your sexual drive, desire, or interest has become flat, absent, or apathetic. Your intimate other will undoubtedly notice too.

Lack of excitement occurs when, despite the desire, your pleasure response to physical or to mental stimulation is absent. The touches, behaviors, and thoughts that used to result in arousal are now not resulting in excitement. Certain sexual dysfunctions are impotence, premature ejaculation, painful intercourse, lack of lubrication, lack of pleasure, and failed orgasm.

You have probably heard it said that the most important sex organ is the brain. Male and female sexual functioning is extremely dependent on attitude and one's mental state. The type of thoughts, positive or negative, you have about yourself, your partner, or about circumstances in your life will frequently determine how satisfying and successful your sexual experience will be. Occasionally, sexual difficulties involve a medical problem, but these problems are often remedied by appropriate medical treatment. A thorough physical examination should always be the first procedure you take when experiencing a sexual dissatisfaction or dysfunction. Find out if your body is in good condition. If you receive a clean bill of health, then you can move on to the second step – checking out your thoughts, feelings, and multiple physical behaviors. Many sexual difficulties are related directly to problems in a person's life or to the unmet emotional needs of at least one of the people in the relationship. Negative thoughts, painful emotions, unresolved hurt, anger, distrust, low self-esteem, depression, and anxiety are all dominant factors that influence sexuality. These negative influences can be between you and your spouse or between you and someone other than your spouse. In either case, unresolved negative influences affect the person you bring to those intimate times in the relationship.

The good news is that these can be worked on. You and your partner are able to address what went wrong to cause painful thoughts and feelings. You can work at forgiveness and at learning to take care of this relationship from now on. Once some of the emotional and mental healing has taken place, then you are ready to gradually re-introduce yourselves to physical stages of trust, intimacy and pleasure. Go slowly. Touch, massage, build on positive and exciting thoughts in your imagination, kiss, find ways to pleasure your partner, be reassuring of one another, and set time aside just to hold each other and gently learn what feels good.

If you want to do some work on improving your sexual life, there are many up-to-date useful reading materials. If you're embarrassed paying for them at the counter, ask your physician or therapist or someone to order them for you. Follow through with all that can be done to make this part of your life satisfying.

Addictions and Somatic Problems

Dependence on and abuse of alcohol, drugs, internet, gambling, spending, food, work, and sex are all critical indicators of major personal or relationship problems. Likewise, sleeping problems or somatic complaints, such a headaches, ulcers, diarrhea, constipation, and neck or back pains can frequently be symptoms of some deep emotional distress, a distress that develops because we are not taking care of our critical emotional needs.

It is critical to know what is physical and what is psychological. The addictive patterns must be seen as illnesses in their own right. If you have one of these problems, it must be addressed as a primary illness, a condition requiring its own treatment, either before you address anything else or at least simultaneously. The seriousness of the condition will determine if it must be dealt with alone or can be treated in conjunction with other issues. If the nature of these problems is medical, not psychological, then receive the appropriate medical treatment. However, if you and your physician rule out medical causes, then you need to look at the state of your emotional needs and commit to psychotherapy.

Other symptoms might include:

- Anxiety and panic attacks
- Impulsive behavior
- Loyalty problems
- Self-criticism
- Unreasonable demands on others
- Concentration problems
- Procrastination
- Irrational fears
- Failure to live up to appropriate expectations
- Hoarding
- Obsessive-compulsive problems

If you've concluded that you're a candidate for immediate hospitalization, relax a minute. We all have many of the above, some of the time. I know that each of us can relate to the checklist of symptoms. The guidelines to determine the seriousness of the symptoms are:

- How often do they happen?
- How long do they hang on?
- How detrimental are they to my daily functioning?

We must keep in mind that we all have some of these symptoms occasionally. We would not be human if we were never depressed, irritable, or frustrated. But, the symptom's frequency, length, and intensity can be the warning signs that something is seriously wrong. If you are not taking proper care of your emotional needs, these kinds of persistent symptoms are your cues, your signs. When you are experiencing these symptoms too frequently, you must pay attention to the fact that you are hurting and probably having some trouble functioning. The symptoms will interfere with and contaminate your personal life, as well as your relationships with others.

The healing is not just in controlling the symptoms. Rather, the healing must be deeper and more inclusive. You must know your six emotional needs; understand them thoroughly as they pertain to you and to your relationships with others, and then learn how to take care of them on your own on a regular basis.

Exercise: Six Emotional Needs

Throughout the next pages, you will be working at learning about your six emotional needs and figuring out what you must do to take care of them on your own or in your relationships with your significant other(s). These exercises are designed to help you look closely at the values and priorities in your life. Feel free to write your responses in the spaces provided or in your personal journal.

1. List the things in your life on which you are very dependent, things you would replace or fix as soon as possible, things you feel you *need* in your daily living. Are you okay with what you see?

2. Walk around your home and price the ten most expensive things you own. How important are these things to your happiness and sense of well-being?

3. Think of the last "sale" you attended. How far did you travel? How long did it take you to get there and back home again? How important was it for you to attend? I want you to think about what things in life get your time and attention.

4. Add up the amount of money you spent on gifts last Christmas.

5. Take 168 hours in a week and break it up into how you spend these hours. What does your week look like as far as what or who gets what amount of your time?

Which of these warning signs are happening in your life?

Depression	Eating to cope
Frustration	Self-criticism
Irritability	Excessive physical problems
Negative thoughts	Overreaction, anger
Emptiness	Concentration problems
Sexual difficulties	Low energy
Using alcohol or drugs to cope	Irrational fears
Erratic, impulsive behavior	Inability to just sit down and relax

Having done these exercises, sit back and ask yourself what your answers mean. A day or two from now, show these questions and answers to someone very close and important to you. Without getting too explanatory or defensive, ask this person what your answers mean to him or her. Listen carefully. Just give this material some thought. Evaluate it yourself, and listen to the feedback from someone else.

As a psychotherapist, people come to me with symptoms that they see as the problems in their lives. These symptoms are very painful, upsetting, and disruptive to daily living. However, these symptoms are warning signs. They are telling us something is wrong. We are not doing something right for ourselves or in our relationship with others. If these symptoms are occurring in your life, you are not adequately taking care of your basic needs. The “dashboard” is all lit up telling you it’s time to pull over and do something!

Spiritual Reflection: Emotional Needs

Scripture:

Read each Scripture passage slowly. Pause between each passage for a couple of minutes. Take a few long gentle breaths. Close your eyes and try as best as you can to still your mind and let any words or phrases you just read cross your mind. Allow the thoughts to come and go. Sit and breathe slowly and gently with the thoughts as they come to you. If a word or phrase seems to stay with you, allow your mind to be still with that thought or phrase. Continue this process with each passage you chose to reflect upon.

- But the fruit of the Spirit is love, joy, peace, patience, kindness, goodness, faithfulness, gentleness, self-control; against such things there is no law. (Galatians 5:22–23)

- I can do all things through him who strengthens me. (Philippians 4:13)

- I therefore, a prisoner for the Lord, urge you to walk in a manner worthy of the calling to which you have been called, with all humility and gentleness, with patience, bearing with one another in love, eager to maintain the unity of the Spirit in the bond of peace. There is one body and one Spirit—just as you were called to the one hope that belongs to your call— one Lord, one faith, one baptism…
  (Ephesians 4:1-32)

- And we know that for those who love God all things work together for good, for those who are called according to his purpose. (Romans 8:28)

Reflection Questions:

Journal, discuss or silently reflect about the following questions:

1. What emotional quality do you want to cultivate more of in your life?

2. What emotional responses toward others show you believe in the value that person has- as God's child?

3. What behaviors and attitudes toward yourself show you believe in the value you have as God's child?

I. SENSE OF SECURITY

Sense of Security

We all recognize the need for such things as water, food, shelter, and money. These basics for daily living are obviously necessary for our physical survival. When I refer to the emotional need of security, these are not the elements of life I am referring to. The *Sense of Security* is the inner peace and comfort that comes from being able to count on or being able to anticipate what is going to happen in our lives. There are four concepts for this sense of security:

- Predictability
- Consistency
- Trust
- Not walking on eggshells

This sense of security in our daily lives is essential if we want to have mental, emotional, and even physical stability and wellness. When the unpredictable occurs, or when something we should have been able to count on does *not* occur, our peacefulness and foundational comfort are shaken. To feel anxious, worried, scared, angry, uneasy, or deceived... these are all very negative emotions. We don't want to live with these kinds of feelings. We also don't like the thoughts that accompany, and can cause, these feelings. For example, we start to have thoughts like:

- If I bring up what I want, I'm afraid that...
- I'm so on eggshells around you.
- Can I really trust you?
- I'm afraid to say anything.
- I think that nothing I ever do is good enough.
- I wonder what has happened to us.
- Can't I count on you?
- If you say you will ... , can I expect it to happen?
- Aren't I important enough that you ... ?
- What's really going on?
- Are you trying to upset me?
- What will happen next?
- I'm feeling so tense and nervous, etc.

When the words or concepts of security are missing in our lives, they might manifest themselves as excessive worry, anxiety, and even panic attacks. In the world we live in, there are times when a sense of not knowing what will happen next is normal and just part of living in a realistic world. At such times, we must have adequate, healthy coping mechanisms. We must be able to deal with and tolerate some of the negatives of life, the uncontrollable times that we can't prevent or change. When we can increase our sense of security, with certain people, we should definitely expect predictability, consistency, and trust.

Some element of predictability in our daily lives is essential. When the unpredictable occurs, the very foundation of our lives can be shaken. This may occur for example, when a young person dies. This is devastating and unexpected and could not have been predicted. In a sense, we can prepare for the deaths of our parents because we know that, in the normal rhythm of life, they are likely to die before we do. But we are never prepared for the death of a child. Children and young people are never prepared for the deaths of their peers. This kind of event can damage the inner security we need to lead stable and emotionally peaceful lives. We can become shaken and experience many conflicted thoughts and feelings. Thankfully, when we have a major crisis in our lives, people tend to rally around us and give us support. But when day-to-day unexpected events occur, we don't necessarily get that support. The cumulative effect of unpredictability is anxiety, nervousness, disappointment, and instability. Let's look at some of these day-to-day events.

One example would be when parents expect children to keep a curfew. If they don't show up, all sorts of negative thoughts go through parents' minds. Parents begin to envision possible events that worry, scare, and anger them. Anxieties grow, and a sense of insecurity builds. Parents need to be able to count on their children, just as children need to be able to count on their parents, to live up to the expectations each has of one another.

This is certainly also very true of spouses. Wives and husbands need to be able to count on and have some sense of consistency and predictability with one another. Although this will be covered in greater depth in the sections on marriage and family, the feeling of safety, that each can bring up whatever they need to with one another, must exist between people in marriage and family life. Spouses and members of a family should not be "walking on eggshells" with one another. People in on-going relationships should be able to clear the air and bring up whatever they need to in order to reach some sense of resolution and inner peace, a sense of security and comfort.

This becomes even more crucial and pronounced when trust has been lost and efforts are being made to regain it. When people have been deceived and let down by a significant other, both people must realize the need to regain trust. This will mean accepting the fact that the person who damaged the trust must accept being checked-up on, being questioned, and accepting any trust-building behaviors their partner needs. The distrusting one needs to check, test, and have time to regain the inner security that comes with being able to trust again. Remember, trust is not a birthright. It is not automatic in relationships. *It must be earned, and when necessary, it must be re-earned.*

Other examples of security involve how consistently others relate to us. If a person we live with or work with is pleasant on Monday but cold on Tuesday, is pleasant on Wednesday but silent on Thursday, this will cause us emotional stress. Such inconsistencies in relationships will take their toll on most of us. What can I count on? What can be expected? Must I approach each day, walking on eggshells, wondering what you will be like today? If there is some stress or pressure going on in your life, must I worry how you will cope and how you will relate to me? Will you take out your stress on me?

It is absolutely unhealthy to be in a "roller-coaster relationship." Never knowing what to expect next or not knowing how so-and-so will react or respond causes unhealthy worry, nervousness, anxiety, and even fear. A person should not allow this to happen in one's life. Later you will read how to assert yourself and how to speak-up in such unhealthy moments. For now, just register that this is not something you should be subjected to and you should be careful not to tolerate what is intolerable.

When people say, “I’m in relationships where I don’t want to say anything when things are going well and I’m afraid to say anything when things are going badly,” one has to wonder how much time they think is left. If someone lives in fear of bringing up a topic, they are definitely causing unhealthy consequences within themself and ultimately within the relationship.

Think of your various relationships – spouse, parent, child, job, friend, neighbor, employer, employee, member of committees – how confident and comfortable are you with bringing up whatever you sense you need to? For example, can you say:

“There’s something I’d like to clear up.”

“May I please mention something that bothered me the other day?”

“You know, I’ve got to tell you it was upsetting to me when…”

“Would it matter to you if what happened the other day really upset me?”

“I’d like to tell you what hurt (or angered, or …) me. Is this okay?

Often, a question is more effective than a statement. There are so many times that people need to resolve what is bothering them. And, when this resolution fails to happen, they are in trouble.

Children definitely need to have some consistency in their lives. What do you think will happen to a child who grows up in a family where daily life seems to have no predictability or consistency? What if the most common feeling is one of tension – “Something feels wrong”? What if there is too much silence or voice tones that say, “I’m upset?” What if the child has no idea who may come home drunk or when the next big fight will happen? Children are certainly in need of some sense of predictability in their lives. When predictability is absent, they may grow into adults who create for themselves and their families the same kind of chaotic, unhealthy pattern they grew up with. They will more than likely have some difficulty with consistency, order, structure, and predictability. Frequently, this will develop into an anxiety disorder or some level of depression.

So very often, children in our society are living with chaotic schedules. There is a constant feeling of hurrying and rushing.

People around them always seem to be getting ready to get somewhere on time. There is an absence of order, calm, and ability to feel relaxed. This is stress! There is definitely a sense of "walking on eggshells" because they realize it wouldn't take much to cause others to get frustrated and angry. There is a sense of waiting to see who is going to lose their temper or create a problem. Everyone seems to be on edge or in a hurry, and everyone seems to have so much going on that there is little or no time left to relax, to be at peace. Think about it, how often do you and your significant others ever hear the words, "You know, we can just sit and relax. We have nothing we must do or need to get done right now"?

It is important not to be unrealistic but to stay in touch with reality. There are some events or situations in life where we do not have the power to exert any influence. There are times in life when we can only cope and realize that insecurity in these situations is a reality. Learning how to live with the heartaches of life over which we have no control, such as the possible unfairness of others, the unsuredness of a job, the health of our parents, and our children's safety on the road are truly challenging, worrisome times which must be faced by mature, healthy people.

We all need to recognize:

1. What is changeable in our lives and should be expected to change?
2. What is changeable but won't be and can be tolerated?
3. What is changeable but won't be, and can't be, tolerated?
4. What is unchangeable but can be tolerated, and one must learn how to tolerate?

This serenity prayer is especially appropriate as we try to deal with these realities:

God, grant me the serenity to accept
What I cannot change;
The courage to change what I can;
And the wisdom to know the difference.

This is not only a prayer; it is also the best definition for mental, emotional, and behavioral health. Let's look more closely at this material and give a few examples of these four points:

1. What is changeable in our lives and should be expected to change?

When stress, anxiety, worry, and hurt come from situations where change should be expected and is achievable, people must be held accountable to do so. Consider the many relationships in which certain changes should be expected. For instance some stresses are caused by a person's disagreeable voice tone, upsetting behaviors, chaotic schedules, or unfair dos and don'ts that dominate the environment of daily living. These are not only changeable; improvements they *should be expected* as part of healthy lives and relationships. It would be unhealthy and damaging to try to tolerate these situations that diminish the quality of life. In this case, choosing to tolerate would be unhealthy enabling. Expect change!

Like what? Think of some specific behaviors of someone in your life that not only upset you and take a toll on you, but are truly very changeable if the other person is motivated and cares how he/she makes you feel. Whatever you come up with should be shared with this person. Make sure you speak gently and softly, either verbally or in writing. Ask the person if they care how they make you feel. Keep in mind that they know there is only one correct answer to this question. Share your concern tactfully, believing you have the right to expect change. Also, be sure this sharing and openness goes the other way as well. Find out what he or she wants *you* to change.

2. What is changeable but won't be and can be tolerated?

To understand this idea, consider these examples. First, bring to mind someone you live with who has a habit that you find upsetting and it puts you on edge. Suppose you recognize that this person isn't likely to change and you believe you are truly able to tolerate the behavior. In this instance, the good in your life together outweighs the bad. You know you are able to cope with the situation.

Another example of when this situation might present itself is in a work setting. Perhaps you believe that the way something is being done or not being done could be improved, if only someone would listen. You may even be in a situation that is downright wrong or unfair. However, in either situation, because you want to keep your job, you decide to tolerate, to live with, what you can't change. This occurs frequently in our society. We can learn to do this without getting an ulcer, becoming depressed or miserable, developing a rage problem, or taking out our emotions on others. Who or what can you identify in your life where your decision to tolerate is an okay decision? The positives in your life and the positives between the two of you make such tolerance a legitimate, healthy choice. Just be clear about these moments, these times, and make sure you're truly being honest with yourself.

To develop a stronger ability to live with these situations it will be important to have:

A. A healthy, strong attitude
B. Helpful outlets – people to talk with, exercise, prayer
C. Be sure other parts of your life are going well and your emotional needs are being met so that you are bringing a pretty content, happy person to these challenging situations

3. What is changeable, but won't be and can't be tolerated?

There are a number of patterns, habits or behaviors that may affect you and could definitely be changed and should be changed, but they involve another person changing. If he or she refuses to make the change, I call this unchangeable because of the refusal to try to change.

So, what behavior patterns are not tolerable and should not be tolerated?

- Verbal and physical abuse
- Drug abuse
- Explosive temperament
- Infidelity
- Refusal to forgive
- Alcoholism
- Refusal to communicate reasonably
- Lying
- Refusal to live up to role expectations
- Gambling addiction
- Pornography

When someone tries to tolerate and to live with these behaviors over a period of time, they will likely experience mental and emotional illness that may take the form of:

- Depression
- Anxiety disorders
- Panic attacks
- Mood swings
- Taking out one's emotions on others
- Physical deterioration
- Turning to one's own coping patterns

A person tolerating these behaviors for too long may develop unhealthy and inappropriate coping mechanisms that further exacerbate the situation. These may include slipping into alcohol or drug abuse, excessive and unhealthy eating habits or damaging innocent others by inappropriately taking one's emotions out on them.

Are any of these intolerable behaviors going on in your life that are taking their toll on you or on your relationship? Can you see where they are even taking a toll on others, such as your children? What do you need to do about it? Is it time to do so? Do you have the strength to do it? Do you need someone to help you do what you need to do? You must find some way to say, "You must change or I won't continue to live this way."

4. What is unchangeable but can be learned to be tolerated?

These situations require an entirely new kind of strength, coping mechanisms, and attitude. Such situations might be illness, death, an unwanted divorce, handicaps, special needs, injury, weather, job loss, death, inability to bear a child, or a past mistake, to name a few. These situations cause a great deal of anxiety, stress, frustration, and sadness. To feel emotionally upset when these occur in our lives is very normal. However, the challenge is to make sure these painful thoughts and feelings don't take over our lives. We work at developing an attitude of tolerance or coping as best we can. We recognize "OK, this is the way it is. This is the hand I've been dealt.

This is as it is and now I need to handle it." Is this easy? Absolutely not! There are times in each of our lives when there is no other healthy choice besides tolerating effectively what has happened or what is. At such times, you must have the determination and strength to move on with your life, to push yourself to make a new life if this is what is necessary.

Take an inventory. Is any person or situation falling into this category for you? How are you doing? If you're having a tough time, why not reach out for some help?

It's very important to inventory your life and figure out if any of those four situations pertain to you. Recognize that all of us can have each of them in our lives at any given moment. We must pay attention to what is changeable and what is not and what we can and cannot tolerate.

How does a person develop this sense of peace? There may be numerous paths. Some include reflection, prayer, and meditation. This may take many forms, both active and contemplative. Each person may find different practices fit them better than others. The important thing is to respect the human spirit that is as much of who we are as our body, mind, and emotions. Our spirit needs care, nourishment, and time to be healthy, which manifests itself in this sense of peace that feeds our sense of security. It is important to take time to honor the work of your spirit on this journey of life.

I want to take this time to talk with you about a problem I see far too often – someone getting their sense of security at the expense of someone else. I will give you five examples of this *inappropriate, unhealthy behavior*. Ask yourself, "Is anyone doing this to me?" "Am I doing this to anyone else?"

The first is **intimidation**. Someone bullies another by threatening statements, physical harm, yelling, name calling and painful silence. Though all of these are unacceptable and should not be tolerated, physical harm is in a pathological category of its own. It is absolutely, unequivocally unacceptable. This behavior should be dealt with and responded to with immediate physical separation. Move out as soon as possible. Do not live within the clutches of physical abuse. Major intensive therapy must be expected of someone who inflicts physical harm. Victims of abuse need to seek the help of a professional or professional support group to make a safety plan and figure out how to implement it in their situation. No one should try to do this alone.

The second example is **control**. A person using control as an attempt at creating their own personal security may convey messages like, "My way or no way." When there is a decision needing to be made or a problem needing to be resolved, the person may ask for someone else's opinion, but in reality, this request has little, if any, value. They have made up their mind. They have already decided what must happen next.

Another example of control is declaring helplessness, creating some level of guilt in another person by claiming, "Without you, what will I do; what will happen to me?" The person feeling controlled, thinks to themselves that they will be doing something wrong by not meeting whatever need the controller is claiming to have. The person feeling controlled must believe that there are other alternatives, other options that can be used. This person must believe that they are not the only answer; that making other arrangements for the person is sufficient caring. There may even be times when the one being controlled may even see the value of reacting in such a way that it forces the "helpless" person to have to react on their own behalf. We frequently refer to this as *tough love.* You might say, "I love and care about you so much that I won't continue to cater to you, and I will start to expect more of you. For both of our sakes, I will not tolerate what you are doing. I will expect changes."

Some other examples of controlling behavior might be:

- Manipulation of money
- The reward of sex or the absence of sex
- The bribery of gifts, of things
- Making false promises, I'll do for you if…

Watch for these various ways of being controlled and of controlling others. They need to be recognized when happening and fought against, objected to. Do not live with them. Do not control others by using them. Inventory others and hold them accountable to stop. Inventory yourself and hold yourself accountable to stop.

A third way of creating one's own unhealthy security is by **physical distance**. Here are some examples:

- Isolation
- Always too busy
- Always gone
- Down in the basement or out in the yard
- Excessive volunteering
- Frequently working late
- On the computer
- In front of the TV

Because of an active or preoccupied life, the distancing partner is not engaged in the relationship. The relationship ends up lacking companionship and depth. The distancing partner feels secure because he or she is focusing on what they want to and on what feels good to them, and they are avoiding what they would find to be an uncomfortable closeness. They are not paying attention to what the other person needs and has a right to expect. For the partner wanting involvement, this results in loneliness, emptiness, resentment, and vulnerability. There can be a strong sense of being rejected or abandoned.

This isn't just a problem in couples' relationships. This can happen in parent/child relationships. Someone who doesn't want to face the demands and expectations of appropriate parenting and of building a meaningful and fulfilling sense of family might avoid them by becoming physically absent. Spouses and members of a family should be dedicated to the prevention of this experience.

This brings us to the fourth example – **shutting down**; silence, not sharing. Someone may be physically present, but really not there. The absence of meaningful communication results in the relationship feeling empty and frequently void of a sense of togetherness. Feeling alone, avoided, confused, and unresolved are characteristics of this relationship. "Talk with me; tell me what you're thinking; help me understand" are the kind of requests that occur from one person to the other. However, the pleading requests are far too often ignored and the loneliness continues. The sense of emptiness is terrible, and the empty person feels powerless as far as what to do about it. The control of the relationship is in the hands of the silent partner.

Finally, a fifth example of a false, unhealthy security, at the expense of others, is **addictive and abusive patterns**. Alcohol, drugs, sex, food, spending, or gambling become destructive ways people use to feel some security or satisfaction in their own lives. Unfortunately, for the addict or the abuser, these methods only work temporarily. They apparently do bring the person some sense of security or satisfaction at the moment. Keep in mind that these are sick, unhealthy methods to escape, cope, or overcome some insecurity. If not addressed and healed, controlled or stopped, they will worsen, and so will the consequences on the other person and on significant others. These particular problems are so critical and so unhealthy that they *demand* a tremendous amount of attention and commitment to therapy. These are some of the major illnesses in our society. If they exist in your life, seek professional help as soon as possible. Call your local Alcohol or Gambling Anonymous program and get direction. If you can't find such a program listed in your area, call your county mental health office.

So far, we have been paying attention to how other people or situations affect our sense of security. It's also very important, and only fair, that you look at yourself. If you see any unhealthy behaviors in your way of living, you've got some work ahead. Start by looking at yourself and address what you must be and do. Ask yourself these questions:

- Do I know what to expect tomorrow?
- Do I have a pretty good idea of how my days will go?
- Do I know where I will be, with whom, and what we'll be doing?
- Am I seen by others as consistent and reliable?
- Do I compromise wellness in my relationship with others?
- Do I listen to others and am I really present to them?
- Do I communicate effectively?
- Am I respectful of another's feelings, needs, or opinions?
- Do I cause others to feel on eggshells?
- Do I have any of those *intolerable* elements in my own life and in my own behavior?

- Do I make it safe for others to talk with me, offer criticism, or disagree with me?
- Am I comfortable to be around?
- Are the people who live with me relaxed and comfortable around me?

How many are "Yes" answers? Do you know yourself well enough and are you honest enough with yourself that you can really answer these questions accurately? How would others answer these about you? Why don't you go ahead and ask them?

Exercise: Sense of Security

Take time to reflect on the sense of security.

1. Who in my life do I worry about too often?

2. Is someone worrying too much about me?

3. Who in my life creates a tension and an anxiety in me because of how they act or react?

4. Do I make anyone feel like they are on eggshells?

5. What situations cause me to be tense and nervous?

6. Where and with whom do I cause tension and nervousness?

7. What practices cultivate a sense of peace for me? Are they healthy for me? How do the practices or patterns of mine affect others?

8. Think of some significant others in your life; are they consistent and predictable?

9. Are you afraid to communicate with anyone? With whom?

10. Does some issue feel unresolved for you? Why?

11. Are you confident that what you have to say matters to others?

12. Are you listened to?

13. Do others believe you listen to them?

14. Is your opinion asked for?

15. Are things ever done your way? Do you always need your way?

16. Are you frustrated and on-edge because someone isn't available to you?

17. Are you as available as you should be?

18. Can you say "no" and it's okay?

19. Can others say "no" to you?

If any of these questions are answered in a way that says there is a problem, I'd like you to write that person and share with them what questions you asked yourself in relationship to them and tell them what answers you had. Then, ask them if it matters to them how you answered. Hopefully, if there is some work and changing needing to be done, the two of you will promise one another to do what needs to be done. Hopefully, this healthy sense of security matters to both of you.

Predictability, consistency, the ability to trust and be trusted and not "living on eggshells" are the concepts that must be lived and experienced for us to have a sense of security. Take time to think about this material in regard to yourself and in regard to your relationships with significant others. Figure out what you must do to be someone others will feel secure around. Figure out what others must do so you feel secure around them and share this with them.

Spiritual Reflection: Sense of Security

Scripture:

Read each Scripture passage slowly. Pause between each passage for a couple of minutes. Take a few long gentle breaths. Close your eyes and try as best as you can to still your mind and let any words or phrases you just read cross your mind. Allow the thoughts to come and go. Sit and breathe slowly and gently with the thoughts as they come to you. If a word or phrase seems to stay with you, allow your mind to be still with that thought or phrase. Continue this process with each passage you chose to reflect upon.

❖ God is our refuge and strength, a very present help in trouble. Therefore we will not fear, though the earth be removed, and though the mountains be carried into the middle of the sea. (Psalm 46:1-2)

❖ There shall no evil befall you, neither shall any plague come near your dwelling. For He shall give his angels charge over you, to keep you in all your ways. They shall bear you up in their hands, lest you dash your foot against a stone. (Psalm 91:1,2)

❖ Fear not; for I am with you: be not dismayed; for I am your God: I will strengthen you; yes I will help you; yes I will uphold you with the right hand of my righteousness. (Isaiah 41:10)

❖ Yes, though I walk through the valley of the shadow of death, I will fear no evil: for You are with me; your rod and your staff they comfort me. (Psalm 23:4)

Reflection Questions:

Journal, discuss or silently reflect about the following questions:

1. What spiritual quality can you cultivate to make you feel more secure in your life?

2. What makes you believe you are secure?

3. Describe feeling secure in a relationship with God.

4. What do you fear? How does your faith help you deal with the fears you feel in life?

II. SENSE OF ACCOMPLISHMENT

Sense of Accomplishment

In Viktor Frankl's book, *Man's Search for Meaning*, he tells the atrocious story of living, dying, and surviving in German concentration camps. While experiencing this horrendous situation, he developed the treatment theory called Logotherapy. Logo comes from the Greek word, *logos*, which means purpose or meaning, and *therapy* referring to a process by which someone gets well. Logotherapy is a therapeutic method emphasizing the need to find meaning and purpose in one's life in order to be well, to survive. He had observed that one major trait that distinguished the survivors from the casualties was the ability to find some sense of purpose and meaning in each day. How? What possible thoughts or attitudes or behaviors could enable someone to make it through such a horrible situation?

- Sharing one's already small portion of food with someone in greater need
- Keeping someone else warm at night
- Praying out loud with others
- Developing an attitude of determination that says, "Survival is a purpose in itself; to survive; to make it through is a victory"
- Deciding that others are depending on you to survive

These thoughts and beliefs gave the person in the camps a sense of meaning and purpose. Though most of us cannot relate to the horrible devastation of the concentration camps, most of us can relate to those times when we wonder if we'll get through certain situations. We wonder if it will ever pass and be over with.

In some ways, there are times in our lives that we experience feelings similar to what Jesus felt during the Passion. Reflect on his suffering and the messages about life, pain, death, and hope we witness in the events of Easter. Think about this for a few minutes in terms of the following ideas:

- Sweating over the fear and anxiety about something happening in our life
- Wishing or praying that it would not happen

- Feeling the pressure and strain in our head, headaches that come with the stress of life
- Having the sense of being treated unfairly ("I find no fault in this man") and being betrayed by one's friends
- The feeling like we're being weighed down by the burdens of life
- The thought that what we are going through feels like a death
- And yet, then there is a rising from it; a moving past it and finding new life

What makes this happen for people? What enables people to survive and get through the tough times and to keep living? It seems it's when they have a sense of meaning and purpose in life greater than the painful period they are going through. They figure out, believe in, and make a life happen that is better than the negative period and the problems that are weighing on them.

Now this second emotional need, the sense of accomplishment, is not just important at times of pain and crisis. It is a need that is important on a daily basis. Meaning, purpose and a sense of accomplishment give us a worthwhile today and an energized tomorrow.

A sense of accomplishment, meaning and purpose comes when we feel pride and satisfaction in who we are and what we are doing. Each of us needs to know that we are contributing and doing something meaningful. You must have places in your life where you end up feeling proud of yourself, pleased that you did what you did. You may be very busy all day, but at the end of the day, if you do not think of yourself as having done something worthwhile then this important emotional need is not being met. "I've been busy all day; however, what do I feel good about?"

Take a minute to write down the things you do on a daily, weekly, and monthly basis that give you a sense of accomplishment, meaning, and purpose. Sometimes people feel sad and disappointed because of how little they are able to say about their own personal sense of accomplishment, meaning and purposefulness.

A sense of accomplishment nourishes feelings of pride and satisfaction in what we can do and who we are. We all need to know that:

I am good at something.
I accomplish something.
I make a difference.
I'm doing something meaningful and worthwhile.

It's important to observe times, places, and ways we feel as if we have accomplished something worthwhile and meaningful. Really acknowledge these times to yourself!

You may be very busy all day long, every day, each week. You may sense that you have absolutely no room on your plate for anything else. Too often, you're actually feeling overwhelmed. And yet, at the end of all this activity, if you don't feel good about it, if you can't sit back and think "nice going, job well done; that was worthwhile;" then you're not getting this emotional need of accomplishment met.

Think of the roles you play in your life – parent, friend, daughter, spouse, son, employee, sister, brother, volunteer, hobbyist, athlete, etc. How satisfied are you with each of these roles? You need to believe that what you are doing is worthwhile and has meaning for yourself and to others. You should believe in and have pride in what you do and who you are. You should be able to list your achievements, skills, and talents. Can you say to yourself, "I am a good, effective mother (or father, daughter, son, wife, husband, etc.)" or "I am consistent in walking a mile every day," or "I keep my home well-organized?" If you have trouble recognizing your accomplishments, then you probably have an emotional deficit in your life that needs to be addressed. This may mean very consciously making yourself focus on some specific way to sense accomplishment. *If it's not there, then create it.*

Years ago a church group of young mothers were meeting for a "Mom's Morning Out." One young woman said that before her baby was born she had an exciting career, but that all she did now was change diapers and clean the house. She was obviously struggling with how she thought and felt about herself and her life. Before I could respond to this comment, a more experienced mother said that she had developed a way to feel successful and worthwhile every day. She said that, in the morning, she listed all the tasks she wanted to accomplish that day. The simplest jobs went on her list, from vacuuming the living room to doing the grocery shopping. After each task was completed, she would mark it off her list. If she did something that was not on the list, she would write it down and then mark if off. At the end of the day, she would look at her list and see how much she had achieved. She said this helped her to end the day with a sense of accomplishment and feeling very good about herself. Also, she began to reinforce within herself <u>the importance of the work she was doing, in terms of the role she was living – a mom</u>! In a culture that does not place as much pride and satisfaction as it should on certain roles, being a good parent and efficient homemaker frequently go unappreciated and ignored or taken for granted by significant others and society as a whole. The mothers began to talk about how essential it was to emphasize the role of parents. (This goes for dads as well). In a society that puts so much importance on a paycheck, career, and what you do outside the home, moms and dads must remind themselves, and each other, of how critically important parenting is and how very important and appreciated homemaking is.

There can be tremendous differences between being busy, making money, having prestige, being involved in many activities, and truly feeling a sense of meaningful accomplishment. What if your job does not feel very fulfilling? You must spend a large piece of your life doing this job, but you sense you need more. Look around - there never seems to be an absence of numerous ways to help others. Tragedies, hard times, people with special needs are constantly around us calling out to us for help. Humanitarian efforts are certainly one way to meet this need of accomplishment and meaning.

However, don't think that caring for others is the only way to fulfill this need. There are numerous ways to achieve this sense of accomplishment on a very personal, self-focused way, and we should not feel selfish or guilty about doing this. Like what? Pause here and ask yourself, "What do I do on a regular basis that I really feel proud of and from which I receive a sense accomplishment and meaning?" Write down what you're thinking about.

Were any of the following on your list?

- Gardening
- Carpentry
- Reading
- Hobbies
- Painting
- Coaching
- Sewing
- Writing
- A committee you're on
- Teaching faith formation
- Making breakfast for my kids
- Holding my child
- Building my children's self esteem
- Being kind to …

If you were unable to make a list or your list seems too short, then you have an obligation, a responsibility to yourself, to explore various options. Search out and try different activities or interests that feel fulfilling to you. Discovering such fulfilling activities may take time and could result in some disappointments. However, be committed and self-determined long enough to find something. Whether it involves other people, or animals, or places (art museum, gardens, volunteering at school, becoming part of a performing arts center), be determined to search and experiment until you discover what you need.

We all need to somehow develop this sense of accomplishment, this sense of pride, this sense of purpose. These thinking patterns and feelings are essential for our personal well-being. We need to recognize, appreciate, and take pride in the contributions we make to our families, social groups, committees, and our work worlds. Now you might be saying, "But in reality, I do not really contribute. I do not do what I should in the relationships that make up my life. I don't do what would seem meaningful." Well, if this is true *you must change it.* If your self-criticism is valid, what are you willing to do about it? You must either learn to appreciate what you are doing or do more so that you can appreciate yourself.

"I'm afraid. I'm uncomfortable where I'm at. I do not know what I'd like to do. Nothing interests me." What thoughts can you think of that stop you from having a sense of accomplishment? Write these out. Seeing them on paper is very important. Whatever these inhibiting thoughts are, they must be fought. You must make yourself *act differently than you feel*.

One of the toughest things we must learn to do is to know when and how to act differently than we feel. When it comes to establishing patterns to achieve a sense of accomplishment, it often requires self-discipline and extra effort. Certainly this determination is influenced by self-esteem. If you continue to live like you currently think and feel, you will remain stuck. You must literally force yourself to follow an action plan and let the more positive thoughts and feelings catch up. That's right, "catch up" because they won't be there when you first start. It's a shame that we don't immediately feel the benefit as soon as we make ourselves do something that is truly good for us. It takes a while for the positive thoughts and feelings to kick in and to become a part of us. However, if you stay with it, they will eventually be there.

You may have gotten yourself into habits over the years, patterns of behaving that you have gotten very used to and comfortable with, maybe even patterns that served some valuable purpose for awhile. For example, being home when the children got home from school every day, volunteering at school, or heading up a scout troop. During those years, these activities may have resulted in a *sense of accomplishment*. What if they no longer do? You must start new ones.

For whatever reasons, you may be very *comfortable* in a role or a pattern that should be changed. It would be wonderful if we were made in such a way that as soon as we did what was healthier for us, we felt great. It would be great if we immediately appreciated the change and felt no discomfort over what we left, stopped, or started. Unfortunately, healthy changes do not immediately feel great. Think of all the healthy choices we can make that may not feel particularly wonderful at the moment we make them:

- Going back to school
- Accepting the challenge of a promotion
- Being willing to join or lead a committee
- Letting go of one role and beginning a new one
- Volunteering
- Restarting a hobby, a talent you once had, recognizing that you may not be as good at it as you used to be
- Stopping an addiction
- Going on a diet
- Exercising
- Having surgery
- Dating
- Attending a support group

Continue to think about difficult choices and changes that you could make to benefit yourself and, if you sustained the effort with them, you would be glad you did.

All of these probably require *acting differently than you feel.* They require a real push from within you. However, it is exactly this type of commitment and effort that is necessary for you to achieve a sense of accomplishment. It is so important that you commit yourself to this effort.

In addition to understanding the role each of us has in maintaining our own sense of accomplishment we should also understand that people in relationships have an impact on each other's sense of accomplishment, and how important it is for people to recognize each other's efforts and needs. When an individual who is important to us fails to appreciate, compliment, or recognize our efforts, this person needs to be held accountable. Being taken for granted or when some effort is unnoticed, these are hurtful moments. If we have a parent, spouse, or friend who tries to dissuade us from our efforts to succeed in something, then that person is not thinking of our emotional needs and our best interest.

These significant others must understand that their support and encouragement and their willingness to help you to achieve what you need to are critical roles for them to play. They also need to be aware of how important their compliments and messages of appreciation are to your sense of meaning. They need to be very conscious of how important it is to say "thank you" and "nice job, sweetheart." These important, significant others need to understand and to accept that there will be times when they need to inconvenience themselves for your sake. They will need to go out of their way to do something that enables you to do what you need to do.

Who in your life needs to understand this? Discuss what specifically they could do that you would find supportive and encouraging. There may even be some attitude, contribution, or behaviors from this significant other that will be absolutely necessary in order for you to do what you need to. Without their efforts, their help and encouragement, you will either be unable to do what you want and need to do or it won't feel right and some pleasure will be lost.

As you work on this particular emotional need, turn it around and find out how you are doing at acknowledging and appreciating others in your life and supporting them in what they need to do for themselves. Always inventory the emotional needs both ways, not just one way.

There is one warning I want to mention in terms of the sense of accomplishment. I just talked about the roles of significant others in your pursuit of accomplishment, meaning, and purpose. As true as this point is, you also want to watch out for where you may be overly dependent on their support, encouragement, and appreciation. There may be times when you must be so determined to do what is appropriate for you that you make it happen on your own. You may need to become creative and assertive to make happen what you need to. You get a babysitter, you work with friends to cover for one another; you carve out some special time for yourself; or you pay someone to do what has to be done so you can do what you need and want to do. You must be healthy and determined. Why? Because taking care of this need for accomplishment is critical to your mental, emotional and physical well-being. It must be balanced – you can't go to the other extreme of being selfish, but you also can't continue to sell yourself short or be sold short by others.

Exercise: Sense of Accomplishment

1. List what you are good at and ways in which you are truly proud of yourself.

2. How often do you participate in activities that give you a sense of accomplishment, meaning and purpose?

3. Can you look into a mirror and say, "You did well?" How do you affirm yourself?

4. Do you structure your life so you can pursue these interests?

5. Do you sense that others appreciate your efforts and accomplishments?

6. Do you frequently feel encouraged by others to pursue your interests?

7. Do you give others the support they need and not take them for granted? As an example, it was amazing how long it took my wife and me to recognize the fact that when I wanted to pursue specific interests of mine, I just did it, while Rosie took care of the kids. However, when Rosie wanted to do something, she had to

make arrangements for a babysitter. We were blind to an obvious inequality. I eventually saw how each of us was stuck in old habits. Men should not take women for granted. Parents should be careful what they are teaching their sons and daughters about being men and women, husbands and wives, dads and moms.

8. Are you overly dependent on the approval or appreciation of others to feel good about what you do? What is necessary and appropriate for you to do?

9. Within the next two weeks, decide that you will make some changes, for your sake. Also commit yourself to sharing what changes need to be made within your relationship with an important person in your life. Discuss how you will work together more effectively as teammates from now on to help and to support one another in achieving each other's need for purpose, meaning and accomplishment.

Spiritual Reflection: Sense of Accomplishment

Read each Scripture passage slowly. Pause between each passage for a couple of minutes. Take a few long gentle breaths. Close your eyes and try as best as you can to still your mind and let any words or phrases you just read cross your mind. Allow the thoughts to come and go. Sit and breathe slowly and gently with the thoughts as they come to you. If a word or phrase seems to stay with you, allow your mind to be still with that thought or phrase. Continue this process with each passage you chose to reflect upon.

- You are the light of the world; a town cannot be hid if built on a hill-top. Nor is a lamp lighted to be put under a bushel, but on the lamp stand; and then it gives light to all in the house. Just so let your light shine before all men, in order that they may see your holy lives and may give glory to your Father who is in Heaven. (Matthew 5:14-16)

- Then Jesus said to His followers, "If people want to follow Me, they must give up the things they want. They must be willing even to give up their lives to follow Me. Those who want to save their lives will give up true life, and those who give up their lives for Me will have true life. It is worth nothing for them to have the whole world if they lose their souls. They could never pay enough to buy back their souls. The Son of Man will come again with His Father's glory and with His angels. At that time, He will reward them for what they have done. (Matthew 16:24-27)

- Whoever wants to become great among you must serve the rest of you like a servant. Whoever wants to become first among you must serve the rest of you like a slave. In the same way, the Son of Man did not come to be served. He came to serve others and to give His life as a ransom for many people. (Matthew 20:26-28)

Reflection Questions:

Journal, discuss or silently reflect about the following questions:

1. What have you accomplished in your life that has lasting value?

2. What do you hope your loved ones would remember about you as the most important value you lived in your life?

3. What have you valued that, as you matured, you came to value less?

4. What have you come to value more?

III. SELF-ESTEEM

Self-Esteem

If one need is more critical than all the others, it is self-esteem. Remember the point that we all need water, food and air? These are critical physical needs. Fatal damage occurs without them. The same is true with our emotional needs. Although all are important; positive self-esteem is the most critical. It is the need that most influences our personal lives and our interpersonal relationships. It is the foundation on which so much of any success in life is based. A person who has positive self-esteem thinks, "I am lovable. I am capable. I am special, and can truly say, 'I like me.'" Can you say these? Do you believe these? When a person thinks these ways about themself and believes these thoughts, they have positive self-esteem. Some of you might be thinking right now that people need to be careful not to be conceited and lost in their self-satisfaction. This is true. We need to be realistic in terms of these positive thoughts about ourselves. Maybe we even need to know how to blend a healthy humility into our thinking. However, our focus here is on a healthy, positive thinking pattern that someone has about himself or herself that results in various feelings and emotions.

What emotions? Emotions like confidence, contentment, and inner peace. Notice the distinction made between your *thoughts* and *beliefs* about yourself and the *emotions* and *feelings* that accompany these thoughts. It is crucial that you pay attention to these two very different functions– your *thoughts and beliefs* and your *emotions and feelings*. *Thoughts* result in *emotions*. Work hard to be aware of this. "What am I thinking? Oh, no wonder I'm feeling this way."

One reason self-esteem is so important is that you cannot start working on a healthy relationship unless each individual in the relationship has a positive regard for himself or herself. All healthy relationships ideally start with two or more participants who basically have a healthy, confident sense of self. This good feeling comes from thinking positively about ourselves; about whom and what we are, and believing it. For example, if you and a partner were taking lessons in doubles tennis and you had a broken leg, your leg would need to heal before the two of you could work together on your tennis game. The same is true for therapy within a marriage or any relationship. If one person is suffering from a disability, like lack of self-esteem, that person cannot work effectively as a member of the team unless he or she first takes care of the self-esteem issues. The unhealthy person needs to be healed so she or he can come to the relationship as a fuller person, capable of focusing on the relationship. More of this will be covered in the chapter on marriage.

Most of us are never totally finished with working on self-esteem. This work will be a constant part of our lives. Whether it is our own personal lives or in our relationships with others, positive self-esteem is foundational. I will discuss this critical topic of self-esteem in various dimensions:

A. What is it?
B. Why is it so important?
C. How is it formed or developed?
D. What can be done about what happened in one's past and what can be done from now on?

A. What is it?

Positive self-esteem is a combination of thoughts, emotions, and behaviors that result in a personal profile that says:

- I have positive thoughts about myself.
- I believe in myself.
- I believe that I am capable.
- I have confidence.
- I recognize my limitations and handle these quite well.
- If my mistakes have had an effect on someone else, I am capable of saying "I'm sorry" and asking for forgiveness and working with them to reconcile what happened.
- I don't put pressure on myself to be perfect.
- I don't put undue pressure on myself to live up to other's unreasonable expectations.
- I believe that I deserve to be respected.
- I value and respect others. It matters to me how I make other people feel.
- I deserve to be treated in certain ways in my relationships with others.
- I handle constructive criticism well.

What other thoughts, feelings, or behaviors are indicative of your self-esteem? The bottom line is that positive self-esteem or negative self-esteem, one way or another, are going on in all events of your life every day. Your self-esteem has a powerful influence on all relationships and how you function on a daily basis.

How would you describe your emotions and feelings?

- I frequently have such emotions as…
- When I think of my daily tasks, I feel…
- When I think of all I must do, I feel…
- When I think I am going to be around other people, I feel…
- Thoughts that most often seem to be going on in my mind are…
- Emotions or feelings that most often seem to be part of me are…

The idea of how powerful a role our thoughts play in causing our feelings is crucial for us to be aware of. Pay attention to how often you say something like, "I feel that you don't like me, I'm not good at it, I won't be able to …" These statements are thoughts, not feelings. These thoughts undoubtedly *cause* your feelings. However, what if the thoughts you're telling yourself aren't true? Think about this. If your thoughts are wrong, you will have the emotions as if the thoughts were true.

B. Why is it so important?

We've looked at what positive self-esteem is. Now let's look at why it's so important. Think about the following statements:

- I am special and valuable.
- I am loveable.
- I am capable.
- I feel confident.
- I can do certain things quite well.
- I like me and believe in me.
- I deserve to be treated with respect.

Think of the contrasting, opposite statements:

- I am not special and have little or no value.
- I am not loveable.
- I am not capable.
- I do not feel confident; I feel nervous and anxious.
- I do not do things well; I am incompetent.
- I don't like me; I don't believe in myself.
- I don't deserve to be treated with respect.

Ouch! Aren't these difficult to read? Think of some people who are very special to you. There is no way you would want them to believe those negative statements about themselves. It is important to realize that all of our roles in life are drastically influenced by the self-esteem we have and by our thoughts about ourselves.

Take a minute to reflect on your roles, relationships, tasks, responsibilities, and activities. Ask yourself, "How are all of these affected by my sense of self-esteem?" Your daily thoughts, moods, relationships, and your daily functioning are tremendously influenced by the thoughts and feelings you have about yourself. Can you understand why positive self-esteem is so important? It is a foundational piece of our existence and identity by which everything else is affected. Sounds pretty important, doesn't it?

Think about how, in each of your roles, your behaviors are influenced by your self-esteem. For example, how strong is your self-esteem when:

- trying something new
- going somewhere by myself
- writing to someone
- being satisfied with a project
- speaking up at a meeting
- applying for a job or a new position
- dressing and taking care of my appearance
- taking care of my body
- observing my sexual attitude and behavior
- observing my personal hygiene
- asserting myself

- having expectations of others
- deciding what I tolerate
- holding others accountable for appropriate expectations
- going shopping
- meeting new people
- sharing my thoughts and emotions
- dating
- public speaking
- reading at church
- keeping my house, my car, my… clean and organized
- observing my ability to forgive and to ask for forgiveness
- saying "hi" to someone in the elevator
- thinking about my upbringing and family life
- thinking about my parents, my school years, someone I dated
- thinking about mistakes I've made

Truly, there is not a facet of your life that is not dramatically influenced by your self-esteem. Certainly, other factors influence our lives also, like priorities, values, morals, cultures, and other people. However, a positive self-esteem is foundational. From it, other elements of our life are influenced!

C. How is Self-Esteem developed?

What if someone told you self-esteem was for sale at Wal-Mart? A smile would cross your face because you would realize "*if only it were that easy*." Developing self-esteem is a life-long process, one requiring much attention and care. Let's look at the beginning of your self-esteem.

Once upon a time, there was a little baby named "you". You came into being as a result of two people being passionately involved with each other. Let's assume that, at least at that moment of sexual intimacy, these two people loved each other and in the expression of their love conceived you. Planned or unplanned, there you were! Gosh, think about it. That passionate interplay involving intercourse, plus nine months of miraculous happenings within the womb, and then the ordeal of delivery… "Hereeeeere's you!"

The majority of the self-esteem formation starts happening at the moment of birth. Once we're out in the world, breathing, hearing, and sensing what's all going on around us, the self-esteem formation is underway. Several factors influence the early development of a person's self-esteem. Reflect on your childhood:

Were you gently cleaned?
Were you dressed comfortably and feeling warm?
What sounds and smells were around you?
Were people glad to see you?
How much holding did you receive?
Were you breast fed or held closely during feeding?
How did older brother(s) and/or sister(s) react?
How long were you in the hospital? Were you at a hospital?
Once home, were mom and dad together?
How did mom and dad talk to each other?
How often were you held, kissed and talked to?
Were you allowed to cry too long? How about not allowed to cry enough?
Did the overall environment and what was going on around you "feel right"?

These factors impact the overall sense of security. Do you think they may also contribute to how someone starts to think about themself?

Few people can recall memories before the age of two, but we can imagine what may have happened in those early years. We can even inquire by asking people questions. Find out what they remember. What pictures have they kept from those years? Are there any pictures? Could the family afford such an activity as making albums? Did anyone write down the first word, the first rollover, the first birthday, the first funny statement? How important do you think any of these are in a person's self esteem development? Since early experiences are probably not remembered, do they impact the person? Certainly! There are no doubts about how significant and influential these developmental years have been for all of us. Our school years and social experiences were critical formational experiences. If these years and experiences were positive, then we are probably fairly positive about ourselves. If they were negative, then we probably struggle with some self-esteem issues, as well as other personal and interpersonal issues. Depending on how negative, how damaging, how absent the positive influences were, they have influenced how big a struggle we have with self-esteem. But, and this is crucial, *you do not have to be defined by your history*. Your history has been powerful, and it has affected you, but old messages can be challenged and undone. You have the ability to make the present and the future be more powerful than your past.

You are definitely capable of changing the beliefs, attitudes, and behaviors that you have learned. You are capable of re-writing these; you can reframe your attitudes; you can learn and free yourself to behave and to react differently. You will probably never totally forget the script that you want to change or de-power. You will probably remember, feel, and want to react at times from the old script. However, you can fight it, change it, and you can write and live a new script! You have a power to change that you may not have realized. It is time to realize it. It is time to do it. Easy? Absolutely not! Possible? Absolutely!

Take note of the people, places, and events that did impact you and have influenced who you are, how you think, how you feel, and how you behave. These were formative. These were defining experiences. However, it is important to repeat- they do not have to define, cripple, or overpower you for the rest of your life. Might they be present to you at times? Yes. Must they define and run your life? No! Present? Probably. Control you? They don't have to.

We can consider the impact our earliest life experiences had on us in combination with more recent experiences and do some significant work on ourselves. All the people and all the experiences have contributed to making us who we are, how we think, how we feel, and how we behave. *They may have defined our past and influenced our present, but they need not determine our future.* If you carry good memories and positive experiences, these you will certainly want to hold onto. On the other hand, if your memories are negative, you will want to depower these influences and change the impact they have had on you. It will be more important to ask yourself if you are holding on to the positive influences on your self-esteem or holding on to the negative ones. Stopping early scripts, how you are used to thinking, feeling, and behaving, is not easy work. However, it is work that can be done. It will be through this understanding that you will know what you must address, what you must work at undoing, and what you must work to create for yourself.

Imagine if we were able to watch a movie entitled, "The (your name) Story," your journey from birth until today, what would the movie look like? Consider the following questions to help you with this imaginative exercise. Think about them or write about them.

Who would be in it?
Who should be in it?
Who would be absent?
What would be happening?
What should be happening?
What would be absent?
What should have been absent?
What messages about yourself were you getting?
Did your family share a religion?
Did your family pray?
What values did you learn?
What morals did you learn?
How was it around the kitchen table?
What feelings and emotions were common in your house?
How did people talk to one another?
How did people interact?
Was the atmosphere positive or negative?
Was the atmosphere relaxed or tense?
Was the atmosphere safe or scary?
Was the atmosphere happy or sad?
Was the atmosphere pleasant or angry?
Was the atmosphere warm or cold?
Was the atmosphere complimentary or not good enough?
Was the atmosphere accepting or critical?
What was it like in your neighborhood?
What was it like at your elementary school?
Would you go to a grade school reunion?
How did you do in school?

Did you have fun?
Did you have friends?
Were you bullied, picked on, or excluded?
Did you grow to believe people liked you?
Were your parents proud of you?
Were friends welcome at your house?
Did your friends like your parents?
Were you mistreated by anyone?
Were you keeping any painful secrets?
Were you living with shame, fear, anger…?
Did you fall asleep peacefully?
Did you cry often?
Was there a lot of arguing and shouting going on around you?
What did you do to have fun?
Did you have fun alone or with others?
What were you proud of?
Were people affectionate and nurturing or distant and aloof?
How did people express love?
What were you good at?
Did you like how you looked?
Were you a bully?
When you started high school, were you confident?
What are your high school memories?
How were your friendships?
Did you date? What kinds of experiences were these?
Did your parents trust you?
Should they have trusted you?
Did your parents attend your activities?
Were you active? If not, why not?
How did people treat you?
How did you treat people?
What was your self-esteem and self-confidence like during your high school years?
Did you get into trouble? What kind of trouble?
What were your morals? Did you live up to your morals?
From 0-18 years old, were you self-disciplined?
Did you act on your feelings?

If we stopped the movie at your 18th birthday or at your high school graduation, what would the movie have said about you? If a thousand people were sitting in the audience and I had just turned off the story and asked, "What do you think about (you)?" What would people say? What would your story, up to age 18, have led people to conclude about you? What do you conclude about you? Are you and the audience seeing a pretty confident, positive, capable, happy, determined, healthy you? Or, are you and the audience sensing someone who has come through these years with some damage? If you see this 18-year-old having some struggles and complications from the journey so far, you have been negatively affected. If you are over 18, then we still have more of your journey to watch. Therefore, let's keep watching until we come to you today.

Was your 18th birthday fun?

Did you have a party?

Did you graduate from high school?

Does this matter to you?

What did your high school years do to you in terms of your confidence, socially, sexually, spiritually?

How secure were you?

Did you have a sense of direction that allowed you to feel hopeful?

What did you do after high school?

What was your sense of identity? Where were you going? Who were you?

From the first 18 years, any struggles with guilt? Resentment? Anger?

Any regrets? "I wish I had…" thoughts? "I wish I had not…"

What were you like at 18 in terms of your thoughts, emotions, and behaviors?

Where were you with significant others? Were you comfortable and at peace?

Was the journey a positive or negative one?

Who was this person that you were taking into the adult years?

What did you do after 18 in terms of education, training, or work?

How did these experiences affect you?

Who was in your life and was the relationship(s) positive or negative; healthy or unhealthy?

Did they help build you or damage you?

Would you want your children, or anyone you love, to repeat your journey, your experiences in their life?

Pause now and think about all the work you have just done. Think of the movie you just watched. Go back over your memories, albums, and significant events. All of these have contributed to the development of your self-esteem. These thoughts and feelings influence the choices you make about your behaviors and the behaviors you accept from others. Truly grasp the significance of all of this.

Read them carefully. Now, what is your conclusion about your own self-esteem? Are you in a good place? Are you fairly strong, confident, and content? Or, do you sense the need to do some healing and strengthening of yourself? Do you realize that some things have happened or not happened over the years that have resulted in a fragile, damaged, unhealthy self-esteem? If so, do not feel hopeless. Do not think nor believe that you are stuck this way. Although difficult work, you are able to build a more confident, strong, healthy self-esteem! It's time to believe in yourself and value who you are.

If you recognize that negative thoughts, beliefs, behaviors, and feelings are getting in the way of your personal contentment and success, or contaminating your relationship with others and the things you want to do, then you've got work to do. You can't redo your history, but you can undo the consequences of it and start a different life. You are able to erase tapes and "record" new ones; you can "tear-up" old scripts of how to live and think and rewrite new ones; you can break old, familiar, and even comfortable but unhealthy behavioral habits and learn to live new ones. You are able to act differently than you think, feel, and are used to acting. Read these last sentences again. You are capable of making changes. You are capable of loving and valuing yourself.

You may be saying right now, "Sure, easy for you to say, but come on, this is not a simple task." Absolutely! This is probably one of the most difficult tasks in being a human being. Undoing old habits of thinking, believing, feeling and behaving requires making major changes in who you are used to being. This is not only difficult work, it is painful. It causes much inner turmoil to change yourself around. It may also create conflict in others in your life who are used to relating to you in one way, and now they also will need to make changes. Ultimately the effort will have been very worthwhile and your hard work will pay off.

Ask anyone who has overcome an unhealthy habit such as smoking, excessive drinking, an eating disorder, or nail-biting, "How easy was it? How quickly was the behavior changed? Were there any consequences or side effects – such as nervousness, sadness, anger, irritability? Was it a tremendous amount of work? How often did they have to *act differently than they felt?* How great did it feel to do the healthy thing?

Going from negative thoughts, feelings, and behaviors to positive ones requires forcing yourself to act differently, to think differently; to reinforce your efforts until at some point the better feelings catch up with the new behaviors and thoughts. For a while, however, doing the "right thing" and making the necessary changes will not feel good. It's a shame that growth – getting healthier, becoming more positive – doesn't feel better while you're doing it. The paradox is that it actually feels better at the moment to keep things as they have been. It feels better or certainly easier not to change. Just as the smoker or drug addict goes through painful withdrawal symptoms in order to change and become free of an unhealthy addiction, the process of becoming well cognitively, emotionally, and behaviorally may feel worse than staying unhealthy – *at least for a while*. Let's look at this more specifically. A person with poor self-esteem struggles with the following:

Asserting oneself and speaking-up
Not tolerating inappropriate behavior
Being self-critical, never good enough
Quick to believe others think negatively about them
Has an excessive need for compliments and approval

Pushing themselves to try something new
Quick to be critical and condescending of others
Experiences social anxiety
Is overly engaged in people pleasing
Having negative thoughts and beliefs about themself
Fails to take pride and comfort in their appearance

D. What can be done about this?

What can you do to build positive self-esteem? What role do others play in building your self-esteem? In Transactional Analysis, we talk about the early tapes and personal scripts that we have developed. Your tapes and scripts are your beliefs and the behaviors that accompany your beliefs. It's like the script in a play. The script tells you about the character you're to play and how to play it. You act out the script. So too in life, we act out the script we have been given and have developed over the years. We have habits of how we relate to others. We have habits of how we let others treat us and what we expect of and from others. We have our personal and interpersonal scripts. Transactional Analysis identifies **four basic scripts**:

I'm okay; you're okay.
I'm okay; you're not okay.
I'm not okay; you're okay.
I'm not okay; you're not okay.

Which script is yours? Think about why you're this way and how it affects your living. Do you wish you had a different script? Which one? Why? In order to make that desired script yours, what do you need to do?

Reflect for a few minutes on your family history. What were your parents like? What script did each of them have? What script did they develop in you and in your siblings? Obviously, they were your role models. What did you learn? What were their beliefs and values in life? How are you like your parents or unlike them? There is no way you could have lived with your parents and significant others and not have been influenced as far as values, priorities, and how to live your life.

Another part of your family life was the formation of some powerful conclusions and beliefs. We all give ourselves messages such as:

What must I do to be a good son or daughter?
My parents are proud of me when I …
When it comes to my siblings and me, I sensed …
My siblings considered me to be …
Life is a success when I …
My being a worthwhile person means I must …
Since I did…
Since I didn't …
My parents' overall attitude about me was …

Self-esteem is associated with self-image. Think for a moment about how you perceive yourself. Are you attractive, interesting, and creative? Or do you see yourself as boring and ordinary? We all have a perception of ourselves, and if that perception is not positive we live with a negative self-image that interferes with everything we try to do and with all the relationships we try to establish.

Positive thinking, complimenting yourself, accepting compliments, consciously shoving out negative thoughts and replacing them with positives, consciously choosing certain actions to do or not do, consciously deciding what behaviors of others will or will not be acceptable, these are all elements involved in developing self-esteem. For some people, this work is not as necessary because they have already developed positive, healthy self-esteem. For others, it is necessary work. It is very hard work, yet, in the end, it will be most rewarding and fulfilling. Please believe me. I personally found the journey from low self-esteem and insecurity to be very difficult and painful. Although I had very loving and caring parents, my elementary school years and peer relationships were very hurtful and damaging. I have known what it's like to need to work at changing thoughts, behaviors, and feelings. I have been with anyone who finds themselves thinking:

- I am not liked.
- I don't fit in.
- Will I get hurt today?

- Will anyone call me?
- Am I able to … ?
- I wonder what that means.
- Are you really glad to see me?

Pretty painful thinking, isn't it? Yes, I know. However, I also want you to believe that you can depower and replace these negative kinds of thoughts. Will the negative thoughts and insecurities ever come back? Probably; they seem to pop up and get in the way periodically. But you can learn to control them better and replace them with positives!

Get ready for the work and efforts necessary to achieve this. You may need to get some professional help to accomplish this. I am so glad that I did. Do not be afraid of this need for help.

Then there is the homework! Yes, homework. You must be committed to setting time aside on a regular basis and think about what you need to do, to believe, and to feel.

Exercise – Self-Esteem

1. Recognize the things that have happened to you in your life, both positive and negative. Highlight and affirm the positives, and identify the negatives. See them as the "enemies within" that you must challenge and replace.

2. Write down the positive thoughts you hold. Read them often. Capture your negative thoughts and beliefs in writing. Beside each one, write the opposite belief, even if you don't believe it.

3. A few times a day, read these positive thoughts and think about what you would need to do in order to believe them. How could you change your perspective? Whose influence would you need to negate?

4. If self-forgiveness is part of your problem, then start dealing with forgiveness. What is it? How do people forgive? Can wonderful people make mistakes? Can mistakes be made for a long time? What steps will I take to forgive?

5. Read valuable self-help books and internalize the solid, healthy messages.

6. If you have a Higher Power relationship, use it. What messages from your Higher Power and faith do you believe in and truly apply to your thoughts and daily living?

7. Take some time to do some work on thoughts, emotions, and behaviors that demonstrate your self-esteem. Write out the thoughts you have about yourself.
    - When I think about myself and who I am, I…
    - I believe I have such positive traits as…
    - The thoughts I have about how I think others think about me are …

8. Now write about your behaviors and actions. Use such statements as: "I can or I can't."
    - I am good at or poor at…
    - I am capable of or incapable of…
    - The things I do really well at are…
    - When I think of my capabilities or skills and compare them to other people.
    - I can…   I can't …
    - I want to be able to…

Look over the writing you just did. Read it carefully and think about what you said about *your thoughts, your emotions, and your behaviors*. Where are you as far as a positive or negative self? On a scale of 0 to 10, what is your *positive self-esteem* score? If you have a score, in your own assessment, of somewhere around 7 or 8, consider that a good self-esteem. A person with 7 or 8 most of the time is in a pretty good place with themself. They not only take good care of themselves, they don't let anyone treat them like they have a score of 2 or less. If this person periodically struggles with those 3-6 thoughts and feelings, they don't stay stuck there very long.

Go back and read again what you wrote about yourself. Read slowly and thoughtfully. Hear the importance of how you think about yourself and what these thoughts cause you to feel. None of us are a 10, at least not for very long or very often. Perfection is not our goal. Perfection isn't realistic. However, an overall sense of self-pride, self-satisfaction, and self-confidence are what we want to achieve. "I hold my head up; I believe in me; I function well; I feel confident; I like who I am; I'm okay." This is what *positive self-esteem* is. So how are you? Are you pleased? Do you need to increase your sense of self-esteem? Do you have some work to do? Get started!

9. Take a few minutes to write an ad as if you were advertising yourself in your local newspaper. This exercise will be especially valuable if you complete this ad before you read the following material.

What does your ad tell you about what you consider valuable about yourself? If your husband or wife or any important person in your life reads this ad, would they know it was you? How would a significant other write an ad about you?

Will the ad emphasize **skills**, as if it were an ad for a job application, or **personal traits**, as if it's an ad for a dating service? Certainly one of these ads is much more personal and vulnerable than the other. If you did the "skills ad," would you be hired? Are you pleased with your competency? Are you proud of yourself and confident someone would want you on their team?

If you did the personal ad, what are your chances of being called? Would *you* call you? Would your special others like your ad and agree with you? What additional positives about you would these people add to your ad?

Notice the many, many ways to use this ad. It has so much value and applicability for personal work, couple work, parent and child work, friendship work. Try it the next time you are about to spend several hours in the car. This should make the travel time very interesting, and hopefully, very beneficial. If you're happy with your responses, then God bless you! Be content and enjoy. If you're not happy, listen carefully; you can do something about it!

The point here is how we see ourselves, how others see us, and how we want to be seen. If you recognize negative thoughts and feelings about yourself that get in the way of your sense of personal contentment or contaminate your relationship with someone else, you have work to do. This work will entail erasing tapes, rewriting scripts, undoing old, familiar, even comfortable habits that are not good for you. The thing I want you to think about and to believe is that whatever may have happened to you or not have happened, whatever negative message you may have internalized about yourself, whatever struggles you may have regarding confidence and self-love, you are able to address and change these on your own and in your relationship with others. Although I don't know you personally, I want you to know you are in my thoughts and prayers as you dedicate yourself to this very important work. I've been there; I understand. Yes, our experiences have been different. You know your own depths of pain and conflict and how much work you may have. *Believe* you can do it and commit to doing it. I am pulling for you!

Spiritual Reflection: Self-Esteem

Read each Scripture passage slowly. Pause between each passage for a couple of minutes. Take a few long gentle breaths. Close your eyes and try as best as you can to still your mind and let any words or phrases you just read cross your mind. Allow the thoughts to come and go. Sit and breathe slowly and gently with the thoughts as they come to you. If a word or phrase seems to stay with you, allow your mind to be still with that thought or phrase. Continue this process with each passage you chose to reflect upon.

- But the Lord said to Samuel, "Do not look on his appearance or on the height of his stature, because I have rejected him. For the Lord sees not as man sees: man looks on the outward appearance, but the Lord looks on the heart." (1 Samuel 16:7)

- Because you are precious in my eyes, and honored, and I love you, I give men in return for you, peoples in exchange for your life. (Isaiah 43:4)

- O Lord, you have searched me and known me! You know when I sit down and when I rise up; you discern my thoughts from afar. You search out my path and my lying down and are acquainted with all my ways. Even before a word is on my tongue, behold, O Lord, you know it altogether. You hem me in, behind and before, and lay your hand upon me. ... (Psalm 139:1-5)

- For you formed my inward parts; you knitted me together in my mother's womb. I praise you, for I am fearfully and wonderfully made. Wonderful are your works; my soul knows it very well. (Psalm 139:13,14)

Reflection Questions:

Journal, discuss or silently reflect about the following questions:

1. Who is someone who makes you feel good about yourself? How do you feel when you are with this person?

2. God created you a good person. Describe your good qualities, abilities, and talents? What do you believe is the best thing about who you are?

3. Who is better off for knowing you and why?

IV. THE NEED FOR RELATIONSHIPS

The Need for Relationships

The majority of us need significant relationships. Travelling the journey alone can make it feel pretty lonely and empty, as well as much more difficult. Although there are some people who seem to do it alone, most of us cannot do this and we need other people to share life with. We're not just talking about a love, marital relationship, and a very intimate and exclusive relationship. We'll talk about this part of our life when we get to the marriage section. At this time, we're referring to family, friends, and colleagues with whom we experience life and share enjoyable, meaningful, and supportive times.

One of the most overwhelming problems people can have in their lives is when they experience loneliness, a sense of isolation, no one to share life with, and no one to turn to. In his book, *I Have Abandoned My Search for Truth, and I am Now Looking for a Good Fantasy*, Ashleigh Brilliant says, "It's a shame if you're homesick while you're living at home." Most of us need to connect our lives with the lives of other people. We need friends who are there when we need them, people we can turn to in a crisis, and just as importantly, people who will share in the fun of our lives. It can be very painful to ask ourselves the following questions:

- Does anybody like me?
- Who wants to know me?
- Who am I important to?
- Who is important to me?
- Who am I close to?
- Who misses me when I am not around?
- Whom do I miss?
- With whom do I have fun?
- When upset, who is around for me to talk with?
- Do people share their personal life with me?
- Are my conversations with others superficial?
- Who can I count on?
- Who really counts on me?
- Where does God fit into my life?
- Do I sense God as a Father?

- Do I sense Jesus as a Brother?
- Do I have a relationship with Mary, the mother of Jesus?
- Do I have a sense of belonging with a church or faith?
- Am I a part of any group?

Before continuing our focus on the need for relationships, we want to underline how important and satisfying we believe a relationship with a Higher Power can be. I am saying this as a therapist, not as a theologian. I am not trying to evangelize. As a clinician, a therapist, I have seen some tremendous differences in the power of the healing process and in finding meaning in life when someone has a relationship with a Higher Power. This relationship may take various forms – God as Father, Jesus as Brother, significant holy figures from history (Mary, saints, prophets, teachers).

Whatever the higher power is, it is important. One of the beautiful healing and strengthening areas of Alcoholics Anonymous is the emphasis they put on the relationship with a power stronger than themselves. Let go and let God, if used in a healthy way, is an effective philosophy for serenity. Take some time to explore this dimension of life. It could be a great source of companionship and a real way to avoid feeling all alone. Such a relationship can put into perspective what happens in life and offer you a great deal of peace. A great book, *Never Alone* by Joseph Girzone. He shares his own journey from loneliness, despondency, and absence of feeling connected to his higher power to rediscovering all of this once again.

When it comes to person-to-person relationships, Barbara Streisand's song, *People,* talks about the two types of relationship needs most of us seem to have. First, she is singing about all of us, "Sisters and brothers" who need one another just because we are people. Then she goes on to sing about those *lovers who are very special people* in their need for each other. We all understand the distinction between the two groups and need to make this separation in our own lives. This chapter deals with non-marital relationships because the second section of this book focuses on couples living out a commitment. At this time, we are going to look at the importance of the intimacy and closeness found in our **friendships**.

The following quote reflects some important insights concerning friendship.

> *Something as precious as our friendship couldn't have been created in just an hour or a day. It's too big and complex for that. In fact, when I think of it, it seems that our friendship is still beginning because I keep finding out new and interesting things about you all the time.*
>
> *The beginning of a friendship... what a beautiful time. A time that we'll remember, maybe not minute-by-minute, but by the feelings that have slowly come out of it.*
>
> *I'm glad that we met and found many reasons to get to know each other better and slowly have become friends. Our beginning has been the beginning of so many kinds of happiness for me.*
>
> --From *For You... Because You're My Friend* published by the C.R. Gibson Company, Norwalk, Connecticut

In our daily lives, the opportunity and ability to share good times with others is truly valuable. We need to be able to connect in a meaningful way with other people. If we cannot, then perhaps we need to look closely at how healthy we actually are as individuals. We need to know that people like us. We need to know that it is important to care about others. We must know how to let ourselves become involved in other people's lives and how and when to let others into our life. If this is missing in your life, you may need to focus on learning social skills, people to people skills, and how to build and maintain close, deeper relationships. Also keep in mind how very important a positive self-esteem is in this relationship building. If you don't like and value yourself, could anyone else?

Most of us have friendships on different levels – comfortable acquaintances, associates, and confidants/best friends with whom we share very personal parts of ourselves. Can you identify these types of friendships in your life? Each type serves a purpose and has its own value. The deeper and more personal a relationship becomes, the more time and effort it may take. Special relationships are a necessity for some people to feel complete. We may be very comfortable with friendships that are characterized by activity, fun, or some specific focus and may not feel the need for intimate sharing, or relationships that have a deeper emotional element to it. If our social needs are met without this level, this is healthy and perfectly okay. What I want to emphasize is that you know yourself well enough to know what you really need and what you're willing to give to develop meaningful relationships. If you're seeking more involvement and sharing in your relationships, then there are things to do to make this happen. Two or more people must be committed to this work for these relationships to happen. It means taking the risk of sharing personal thoughts and feelings. It means being willing to become healthily dependent on someone else and let them be healthily dependent on you. It means being willing and able to work at understanding, communicating and problem solving some of the more personal challenges in our lives and involving others in the process. It means knowing when and how to be sorry, how to forgive, and how to move on, and remaining truly significant to one another.

For many of us there is a desire to be able to connect in a meaningful way with other people, and if we cannot, then perhaps we ought to look closely at what thoughts and fears we are harboring. If we want people to like us for ourselves, then we must be able to let them know who we really are. We must share and talk about our deeper selves and risk exposing our thoughts, fears, feelings, and wishes. This sharing determines how involved with one another we will be. I am hoping you realize you have choices when it comes to relationships and how deep and intimate you want them to be. If you recognize that you want something you're having trouble creating or maintaining, then you probably have some work to do learning how to share, to open yourself up, to ask questions of others and create depth.

How do you initially come across to people? Do you initiate activities or wait for someone else to start them? Have you learned how to ask questions to motivate others to talk and share about themselves? Are you a good listener? Do you come across as interested? Are you willing to talk on a deep, personal level, or do you prefer to keep conversations somewhat superficial? Can you pick up on someone's emotions and convey that you understand? Do you share your thoughts and emotions freely? These are skills you can work on and learn.

When you are going through a crisis, it is important not to isolate yourself. For instance, people going through very painful times frequently cut themselves off from their friends and family, just when they actually need their support the most. Most communities offer a wide range of support groups for people experiencing crisis and these groups are very helpful. Plus, by reaching out for help and support, and by giving help and support, people create the opportunity for significant relationships.

We always need to be careful not to let helping relationships become unhealthy dependencies. There is a definite difference between a healthy dependency and an unhealthy one. Let's talk about this in a little more detail. This is an important concept to be clear about. In Transactional Analysis, we talk about the unhealthy triangle that requires two people to play different roles.

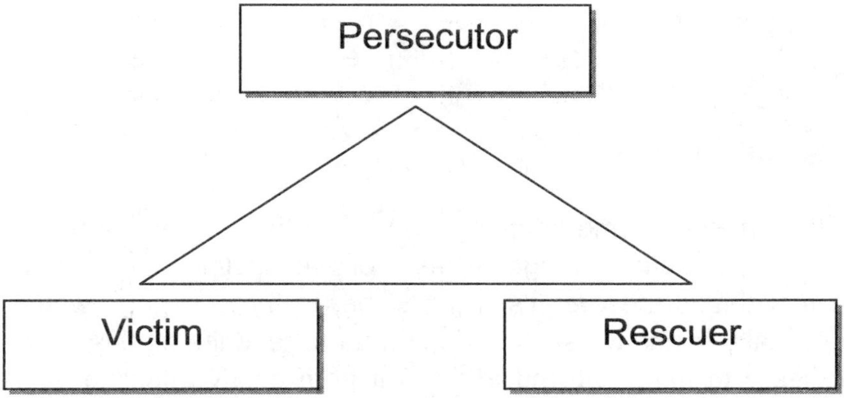

One person seems to be in a great deal of trouble. They always seem to be struggling with life. You sense the risk involved in asking this person, "How are you doing?" because it usually results in a flood of problems and needs. Often times, they are the same problems and needs you heard the last time you asked. They believe various persons, events, or situations in their life are “persecuting” them. This person certainly seems to be in a victim position. If the other person, the rescuer, is caught in this unhealthy interplay, their response is one of offering advice, assistance, and emotional concern. However, these efforts never result in any effective improvement for the “victim.” As a matter of fact, the victim seems to usually indicate that the “rescuer’s” efforts never prove to be satisfying or truly valuable. Consequently, it doesn’t take too long before the rescuer begins to feel like a victim and begins to see the victim as a persecutor. Victims feel as if nothing is ever right; no one can truly understand, much less help, and that things will never improve. For them, life is an experience of the glass half empty versus half full. And even when the problems are quite real, the message seems to be to wallow in them versus to change them or to cope with them more effectively. Others who share time with this person experience quite a collection of negatives:

- Pity for
- Sadness about
- Want to help but doesn’t seem to help
- Helplessness
- Guilt
- Resentment
- Anger
- Disgust
- Desire to avoid

There may be some people in your life with whom you tolerate the situation, because of age, illness, or life circumstances. You *decide* that this is the way it’s going to be; to try to change would probably make things worse; you don’t want to “end life on this note” so you learn to handle it and to keep it from overly affecting you. Really evaluate if you are making the right decisions. Don’t rule out “tough love.” On your own and with significant others make sure you have coping mechanisms in place. For sure, keep in mind the power and wellness of the Serenity Prayer.

God grant me the serenity to
accept the things I cannot change;
courage to change the things I can;
and wisdom to know the difference.

One of the best ways to deepen a friendship is to directly admit your needs. You might say to a friend, "You know, I'm feeling really lonely and I'd love to go to a movie with you," or "I'm struggling with a problem I'd like to discuss with you." You have to learn that reaching out and admitting your need for people is okay. Wanting to have something quite special between the two of you is truly a beautiful, unique experience. This can be very different from the unhealthy triangle.

This gets difficult when the need is not mutual, or if one of you has a stronger need for a certain level and depth of friendship that the other doesn't have. You are risking rejection, but it may be time to reevaluate that friendship and not take this risk. Of course this relationship effort goes in reverse as well. It is important for you to be receptive to your friends when they are in need. A serious relationship needs to be a two-way street. If it is one-way too often, it is probably not going to last very long. If it does last, it will probably become an, "I'll take care of you" relationship and eventually stops being a friendship. What will it be? Healthy dependency versus unhealthy? Close versus too close? It's important for you and another person to find *balance* by talking, experiencing life together, and sharing thoughts and feelings. Find out if you have similar needs and energy. Explore if the two of you are looking for and capable of a similar level of intimacy and closeness.

Some of the More Difficult Times in a Relationship

On the other hand, we must look at what to do when we're not okay. Think of someone in your life with whom you feel uncomfortable, unresolved, let down, angry… with whom something doesn't feel right. Take your time on this and make a list of people with whom you wish it felt different.

- You haven't resolved or worked something out
- Something has changed
- Certain feelings need to be addressed
- You sense a distance
- A conflict has occurred and you haven't successfully healed the issue together

Unresolved relationship pain can exhibit itself as anger, tension, resentment, misunderstanding, jealousy, conflict, or changes in priorities. To resolve it means talking something through to the point where both parties are able to say they cleared it up, or apologized and found forgiveness, or were able and willing to accept something being different but wanting to move on together anyway. In any of these situations, the people have talked, listened to each other, and were willing to care more about each other's feelings than on being right. They were able to say to each other that their relationship from now on is more important than yesterday. *They don't minimize* the other's thoughts and feelings; *they don't deny* their own emotions and pain; *they don't pretend* that nothing happened. Instead, they acknowledge their feelings and admit to whatever they have been struggling with, but make clear the message of missing each other and wanting to be back together again are much more important than needing one person to be right and the other wrong.

Specifically, how do people heal and grow back together? What do the two of them need to be able to do? Let me describe some of the skills and attitudes people must have to re-connect their relationships.

- Each must have the belief that this relationship is important to them.

- Each must consider the relationship more important than the past events, statements, emotions, or whatever happened.
- Each must be more concerned about one another's feelings than being right.
- If conversation does not result in reaching a mutual understanding and awareness that wasn't there before, then they both are able to agree to disagree and declare that being together is more important.
- If one does need to take ownership for having hurt the other or for having caused some pain to the other, this person does so with a sense of sorrow and the other is capable of forgiving and putting the event behind. This doesn't mean you never think of it. It means you can quit bringing it up and when you think of it, you find ways within yourself to not go there again. You move on with the attitude of "from now on."
- They both take on responsibility for getting together in person, by phone, or in writing. Each is not waiting for the other to begin. Someone just starts it.
- They must have communication skills or at least make communication efforts. This means they express themselves, listen intently, and respond. You are making sure to hear what the other meant to say. You also make sure the other is hearing what you meant to say.
- Each must be emotionally sensitive. This means there is the awareness of one's own emotions and feelings, as well as being able to be aware of the other's emotions. Quite often it's more important to pay attention to how someone is feeling versus focusing on the words. I'm not minimizing how important it is for people to learn to say what they mean. This is very important. It's just that, at times, some people's emotions come across more clearly than their words. Be sensitive to this.
- Someone might need to decide on their own that they don't need to bring an issue up again. They can put whatever it is behind them and focus on "from now on."

This last point can be an extremely difficult thing to do. A person may be convinced that they were treated badly and their hurts or angers are valid and justified. They may believe they deserve an apology. Perhaps these are all correct. However, for various reasons, they know they're not going to get what they think they're entitled to. This really leads to a number of questions:

1. Can the two of you still have a special relationship?
2. Could you at least continue a cordial, friendly relationship?
3. Do you need to make a friendly relationship happen for the sake of other people? Are you willing and able to do this?

What we're looking for here is what circumstances warrant making efforts to maintain some level of comfort in the relationship? Figuring out when to make efforts to heal versus make efforts to get along versus needing to say goodbye are tremendously challenging options in relationships. So many people can be affected by whatever option is chosen. Before deciding, it is best to get some input from others, possibly even professional advice.

As you can see, meaningful, deeper relationships take time and work. As wonderful and as easy as some of our relationships do feel at times, there are also times when it isn't easy to work on relationships. This effort certainly falls under the emotional need of Taking Care of Unfinished Business, which we will be dealing with shortly. These two emotional needs certainly intertwine with one another. As we look at one of them, we must at the same time understand the significance of the other. They dove-tail with each other.

If you have significant and meaningful relationships, see them as blessings. Maintain them with openness and sharing. Be committed to any work they may take, and find ways to acknowledge them. Don't take them for granted. Acknowledge to these people, verbally or in writing, that they are truly a significant, necessary, and wonderful part of your journey.

The point of this chapter has been to figure out how important significant relationships are for your well-being. Significant relationships are ones with depth, sharing, feelings, understanding, availability to one another, openness, sorrow, forgiveness, compliments, expressed appreciation, trust, and nurturing, to name a few. What more can you add? It's important to recognize that these relationships will, at times, require work and effort. I've mentioned what some of this work and effort will look like. Hopefully, you will succeed and be at peace with the efforts you make.

Exercise: The Need for Relationships

Take a few minutes at this time and work on the following exercises.

1. The people I am truly blessed with having had in my life and/or with having in my life: Whom can you list?

2. Do they know you think this way about them?

3. When is the last time you told them?

4. Do you want to tell them in the near future?

5. How will you do it?

6. If they asked you to be specific as to why you regard them as so special, what would you say?

7. Which people consider you to be a significant, special friend in their life?

8. How do you know this?

9. When is the last time they told you?

10. Do you want them to tell you?

11. How will you let them know?

12. If you asked them to be specific as to why you are special to them, what would they say?

13. Are there some people for whom there is distance or a discomfort, and you want to make a healing effort?

14. Should an effort be made, or just leave it alone? If you leave it alone, will you be okay? Will significant others be okay?

Spiritual Reflection: The Need for Relationships

Read each Scripture passage slowly. Pause between each passage for a couple of minutes. Take a few long gentle breaths. Close your eyes and try as best as you can to still your mind and let any words or phrases you just read cross your mind. Allow the thoughts to come and go. Sit and breathe slowly and gently with the thoughts as they come to you. If a word or phrase seems to stay with you, allow your mind to be still with that thought or phrase. Continue this process with each passage you chose to reflect upon.

❖ Jesus replied: "Love the Lord your God with all your heart and with all your soul and with all your mind." This is the first and greatest commandment. And the second is like it: "Love your neighbor as yourself." (Matthew 22:37-39)

❖ But love your enemies, do good to them, and lend to them without expecting to get anything back. Then your reward will be great, and you will be sons of the Most High, because he is kind to the ungrateful and wicked. (Luke 6:35)

❖ Do not judge, and you will not be judged. Do not condemn, and you will not be condemned. (Luke 6:37)

Reflection Questions:

Journal, discuss or silently reflect about the following questions:

1. Who taught you something significant about relationships? What did they teach you?

2. What is an experience you have had of loving another that is important to you?

3. Who has forgiven you? What did that mean for you?

4. Is there anyone you want to get closer to? How will you go about deepening your relationship?

V. UNFINISHED BUSINESS

Unfinished Business

Back in 1973, I was participating in a training weekend for Transactional Analysis. This treatment philosophy emphasizes such concepts as "I'm okay, you're okay;" the power of having a life script and what you can do with it; and the parts of us called Parent, Adult and Child. This weekend took place Friday through Sunday. On Friday, we began by telling the group about our family backgrounds. Later that evening, while I was driving home, I began to cry. It felt like a very deep, childlike cry. I let myself go through this for a while and when I stopped, I wondered what had triggered the tears. I recalled that earlier in the evening I had shared with the group how I had really missed out on a close relationship with my dad because I had moved out of my home at the age of 14, when I entered the seminary. My mom and I had always been quite close, but I felt a distance with my dad on an *expressive level*. I knew he loved me. I just needed more in the expression of it. I saw him as a wonderful dad who did many things with me – played catch, took me to cowboy movies, and someone who attended all my activities. However, I felt the need for some verbal and physical expressions of love.

I remember how I could score 30 points in a varsity basketball game and dad would come to me after the game and say, "Duker, you played a great game. But remember that free throw you missed? Next time, loft it just a little more." He meant well, it just felt like bad timing. I knew in my head that my dad was proud of me and loved me, but since I felt some emptiness and sadness, I needed some more affirmation. Something was unresolved, unfinished, and missing between dad and me.

I went back to the class on Saturday morning and told them what happened to me on the way home. I promised I would meet with my dad within two weeks to try and finish what needed to be finished, and perhaps start what needed to be started.

The following week, I phoned my dad and asked him to come over when he and I could be alone in my home. When he arrived, I began by saying, "Dad, I need you to help me work through something." I told him I did not want to hear about my brother and sister. I did not want him to talk about "you kids," I wanted him to talk about **me**, to tell me what I did that made him proud, to tell me that he loved me specifically. I asked him to hold me. There we were – a 30-year-old man being held up by his 70-year-old father while sitting on the couch. I snuggled up in his arms like a young child. Although at first feeling some embarrassment, it didn't take long for me to sense that he was really quite okay with this, and so, I was able to just relax, be okay, and enjoy it also. It was a wonderful experience and now a wonderful memory.

From that day on, my dad and I had a much closer, more affectionate, more satisfying relationship. I wish I could do that again today. However, since he and mom are in Heaven, I have to settle for just talking to them. The holding will have to wait. But, it was truly a significant turning point in our relationship because from that day on, we could verbally and physically demonstrate our love for one another. Because dad *heard me* and *was willing and able to do something* about what he heard, the unfinished business changed in truly the most ideal way. As a matter of fact, he must have realized that the day would come when he would no longer be there to remind me about how he felt and thought, so he took the opportunity one day to write to me on a little card, one you know I will keep forever.

> Dear Duker,
>
> A proud father is now at the helm. I am as proud as a peacock because of the love you and your family have given us. You are tops in my book and you will always be that way to me. No greater love can a Father have than I have for you.
>
> Love,
>
> Your Dad

My dad knew I would treasure this card and I'd read it often. It doesn't matter how much time goes by, whenever I read this wonderful note from him I tear-up and feel very strong emotions. Just think what I would have missed out on if I had not asked for what I needed. If I had not arranged that time with him, all the joy that has come from that invitation would have never occurred. I am so thankful that I was assertive enough to commit myself to that effort and that I followed through. It's important for me to say something regarding this wonderful event with my dad. You might be thinking that not everyone would be able to make sure such a wonderful event would occur. You're right! It is sad that more efforts of this nature wouldn't result in the same way. A part of me knew it was safe to ask my dad to be there for me. I truly understand that everyone can't do this, or the risk to try it is much higher. I'm with you, and we'll address this shortly.

Think of the people from whom you would want such a note.

- Do they know you would want it?
- If you asked, would they respond?
- What's wrong with asking for it? Don't get stuck on the thought, "If I have to ask, then it won't be sincere."
- Will you ask? Will you tell them my story and add how wonderful it would be for you if he or she would...
- What about the other way? Who in your life would treasure such a note from you?
- What are you going to do about it?
- Who needs you to hold or to hug them?

Notice how we cannot look at the emotional need of unfinished business without the likelihood of also touching on the need of relationships. As you work on one of these needs, you will oftentimes also be working on the other one as well.

This experience with my dad is a very good example of taking care of unfinished business. In this case, it is called interpersonal unfinished business because it was between me and someone else. There is also another type of unfinished business - personal unfinished business, just by yourself. The emotional need – taking care of unfinished business can be

A) Personal

B) Interpersonal

Some common unfinished business issues include:

- Neglect, absence of needs
- Abuse – physically, emotionally, sexually

- Never having heard positive, loving affirmations
- Too often hearing negatives
- Rejections
- Betrayals
- A traumatic incident or experience
- An unfairness happened (being lied about)
- Some personal failure, regret, guilt, mistake
- Never thinking you were ever good enough
- Being bullied
- Being cheated on

The emphasis here is that there can be personal or interpersonal unfinished business. These times can involve a personal regret or healing you may need to go through primarily by yourself. Other times, it can necessitate involvement with someone else. This unfinished business might be insuring someone of a positive wonderful message, or it might require clarifying, forgiving, and healing from an experience. In both types – personal and interpersonal – the goal is to reach some inner peace, personally or with someone else.

Personal Unfinished Business

Let's start by looking at personal unfinished business. As we are living our journey and experiencing life in the many roles we take on, we need to first look at ourselves and our own personal readiness to live healthily before we focus on others. It is so much easier to see what's wrong with someone else, to see how they complicate our life rather than to look at ourselves.

> Why look at the speck in your brother's eye when you miss the plank in your own?
> (*Matthew 7:3-4)*

> How can you say to your brother, 'Let me take that speck out of your eye', while all the time the plank remains in your own?" (*Matthew 7:4-5)*

You hypocrite! Remove the plank from your own eye first; then you will see clearly to take the speck from your brother's eye."
(*Matthew 7:5-6*)

I entered the seminary at the age of 14. Eight years later, I graduated from college with the readiness for the journey of life and maturity of a 14-year-old. Despite the many positives from my years in the seminary, there were various personal developmental tasks and life skills that I had failed to learn. I wasn't, as a young man, where I needed to be. Certain maturities, strengths, disciplines, understandings, life skills, and inner qualities were missing in me. It was like missing out of the eight years of elementary school and jumping right into high school. This wouldn't work. Consequently, some of the problems, difficulties, and challenges in my life were happening, not because of other people and events, but because of my own personal unfinished business. There were significant and multiple areas of maturity and life readiness that I had to work on and to develop in myself.

This is an extremely important concept. So often, as a therapist, I see people whose life isn't going the way they think it should, and they want to focus on others. They want to look at their parents, their kids, their jobs, their spouse, their friends, their boss, their colleagues . . . the system they are caught in. They want to find answers and blame outside of themselves. They certainly don't seem to want to start with self.

In my case, I found myself in different roles with their corresponding demands and expectations, and I was not ready for them. *Personal readiness* is so important. What does it mean to be personally ready to take on the roles of life as a person, a partner, and a parent? Whatever roles of life we get ourselves into, the fact is, if we are to succeed in these roles we must be ready and capable of succeeding. We must be personally ready.

In the vast majority of roles we get into during our life, we must prove ourselves. We must have had a certain education. We must have had certain experiences. We must have certain skills to make the team. We must prove we're ready and capable. And yet, in this society, we can get ourselves into the most demanding, challenging, and crucial roles of life – an independent person; a partner in marriage; a parent responsible for children – and not be ready! It is pretty scary to be in such crucial roles and have such responsibilities, and not to be ready.

I found myself realizing in the mid-80's when I was in my mid-40's that I had missed out on a crucial period of healthy growth and development from 14 to 22 years old. There I was, an independent person, a partner, and a parent, and I had to back-up within myself and examine and develop the traits of maturity, stability, and wellness in order to succeed in all the roles I was in. The inner struggles were primarily within me, not from the outside or with others. They were mine and the work had to begin with me. This is where any therapy must begin – asking ourselves if we are okay. As a person, I must start with my own assessment. Who am I? How am I? Am I ready for whatever I am doing? Am I thinking, behaving, feeling, and making choices like a stable, healthy, mature person? I must start with myself.

Some of the more painful personal unfinished business issues some people have to deal with are:

- mistakes and regrets from youth and early adulthood
- having taken advantage of someone
- gave into some level of immorality and selfishness
- hurting someone physically or emotionally
- abortion
- having had an affair
- having given in to others' demands and selfish needs
- financial mistakes

Whatever these may have been, how long must they interfere with moving on in one's life? To forget them is impossible. However, to forgive oneself for them and be able to think and feel good about oneself again are very possible and should happen. Remember, good people *make* mistakes, even serious ones. Good people can *learn* from their mistakes. Good people *grow* from their mistakes and *stop making* the same mistakes. Perhaps you will be able to help someone struggling with similar mistakes and pains.

A very wise mentor and therapist of mine once used the metaphor of a stone representing a failure, regret, or mistake. Close one eye and hold the stone over the other eye. Now you can see nothing but the stone, but if you set the stone down and look at it from a distance, you see much more than the stone. Don't let a stone blind you from setting it aside and see the rest of your life journey.

Meditate on this image as it applies to you. Picture it; identify persons, places, and events. Put them on the pile. Realize we get lost, discover a detour, hit a pothole, and stumble as we journey in life. And then, we can get back on the right road. Let the painful, regrettable mistakes of life be seen as wake-up calls to learn from, to grow from, and move on from.

This brings up the huge topic of *forgiveness,* the ability to forgive self, to forgive another, and to be forgiven. What does "forgiving yourself, forgiving someone else, and being forgiven" mean to you?

What about this definition:

> *Forgiveness is the combination of thoughts that lead to an attitude where someone is able to look at some painful mistake that was made*
>
> ***and***
>
> *to look at the person who made the mistake*
>
> ***and***
>
> - *No longer resent this person*
> - *Be able to see value in the person*
> - *Be able to recognize that good people made mistakes*
> - *Want the person to be able to value themselves*
> - *Want the person to believe he can stop being stuck in guilt*
> - *Want the person to be able to move on with living*
> - *Not need to bring up the painful event, or bring it up with care and gentleness*

Whatever the unfinished business, I believe we each know we must make the efforts to address this need. We must be committed to making cognitive, healing efforts so we can achieve greater inner peace and be able to say, “I am doing a good job at taking care of my personal unfinished business.”

Interpersonal Unfinished Business

Having spent a good amount of time on personal unfinished business, we are now ready to move on to interpersonal unfinished business. While we must accept that certain relationships are not significant enough to put a great deal of energy into, there are some that absolutely should not be ignored. Which ones? Parents, siblings, spouses, children, certain friendships, maybe colleagues, teammates, committee members, and our God. In these relationships, when unfinished business exists, it is not long before negative consequences set in. The consequences will be both personal and interpersonal. Paying attention to one's *own* unfinished business always remains a priority, but how effectively we deal with one another and how effectively we communicate through past and present issues become crucial issues for healthy living.

Unfinished business is when there exists inside of you a sense of "something doesn't feel right or hasn't been worked out" in your relationship with someone else, past or present. It's an awareness that between you and someone else something doesn't seem resolved, comfortable, or reconciled. How you want the relationship to be from now on needs to be worked on. When someone lives with unfinished business, they may experience such symptoms as:

- a free-floating, frequently present sadness
- nervousness
- over-reacting to things
- anxiousness about what's next
- irritability and anger
- resentment
- sleep disturbance
- sexual problems
- a feeling of unsettledness
- moodiness
- turning to unhealthy behavior to avoid thoughts and feelings
- regret
- guilt
- getting into trouble
- a sense of being uncomfortable, on eggshells
- preoccupied

The point is, on a conscious level, there is a sense of uneasiness, unsettledness, or something feeling not quite right. On an unconscious level, a person may experience symptoms and not be aware that the source is some unfinished business. To bring the issue to a conscious level, we need to ask a number of questions about people, places, and events, and pay attention to our reactions. For example – a commercial, a song, an article, or a picture that make us cry, get angry, or experience some other surprising reaction should remind us that we've got something going on that we need to pay attention to.

There are several ways unfinished business with others can be an issue.

A) It is possible to have some important unfinished business with *someone who is no longer living.* If you have religious beliefs that include an afterlife, you probably believe you can still reach this person and this can be very comforting. If in heaven, you know they now have the wisdom, understanding, and caring desire to help you in whatever way you may need their help. Though you obviously cannot communicate directly, you can still work this through symbolically. You can write the person a letter and then burn it or throw it in the ocean or keep it to read occasionally. You can talk to the person at the grave site, in your living room, on a walk, or while looking at their photo. You know this person well enough that you probably know what they would say or how they would react if they were actually with you. Go ahead and tell them you have some things you need to say and you want them to understand. If you believe you'll see them someday, tell them that you're not going to keep carrying the issue around anymore and letting it bother you so much. Rather, you're giving yourself permission to "put if off" until the two of you meet again. But, in the meantime you need to get on feeling less burdened.

If you don't have this after-life conviction, have the dialogue anyway. Pull out a photo and talk to it. Imagine the person sitting in the room with you. Think about and talk to the person about mistakes we have made, how we have let each other down or failed to take care of what needed to be taken care of. Talk about how we didn't say those things we wish we would have said or not said at the time. The point is that you do not ignore this unfinished business, even if the person is no longer living. You may need to release negative memories, express sorrow, or offer forgiveness. Maybe you might share a late "thank you" or a message of love. Whether positive or negative, give yourself permission to let it out. If it's long overdue positive messages, feel joy. If it's long overdue sorrow or forgiveness, feel relief and closure. If it's long overdue rage, resentment, and hurt, and you're unable to find peaceful satisfaction, respect your negative thoughts and feelings and feel entitlement. If this process doesn't bring relief, seek some help from a professional therapist. At least question if it's good for you to leave it this way.

B) The second kind of unfinished business with someone else is when the person is still living and the unfinished business has to do with something that happened in the past, perhaps years. The event might have happened during your childhood, adolescence, or early adulthood. It might be something you experienced while on your honeymoon, the day you delivered a baby, or in the breakup of your marriage. Perhaps an event continues to bother you or you regret something said or not said, done or not done. It continues to have a negative effect on you. You are aware of some of these feelings:

- preoccupied, bothered
- moody
- angry and irritable; resentful
- unresolved thoughts and feelings
- over reacting
- uneasy, uncomfortable, on eggshells
- disappointed
- hurt, sad
- a sense of "we never worked that out" or "I never told you that…"

These signs are indicative of the fact that someone or something continues to bother you today, although the incident goes back months or even years. You're not at peace with the person or the event. You don't have a sense of resolution with the person and whatever happened or didn't happen. You have some work to do to become more at peace in your relationship with this person over whatever incident bothers you.

What sort of work? It means you need to address some things with someone else to lessen the negative thoughts and feelings that exist between the two of you. How can we accomplish this?

1). If the issue is with a person, someone must care enough to initiate the discussion. Someone must decide that, whatever is wrong, it is important enough to do something about it.

2). We must decide on the way to communicate with the other person – face-to-face, a phone call, or a letter? The letter method seems best for many reasons.

   a. The initiator can truly think through what he or she wants to say and be clear and concise.
   b. The receiver has time to read and to reread without feeling any pressure from someone being right in front of them.
   c. Both parties have a chance to see if the receiver has a similar motivation and concern as the initiator and truly wants to work at healing. If so, the receiver can now decide on the best method to respond.

For resolution to occur, the people involved may not need to agree on the historical details. To argue over the details each recalls may reach a point where they decide that agreeing on the details is not important but that caring how each person felt does matter. Effective phrases might be:

- I've always wanted to tell you that…
- I am sorry
- I wish I could do it over or differently
- What can I say or do for you now?
- Please forgive me
- I understand how hurt or angry you were
- Can we put that behind us?
- I'll try to never do that again
- Thanks for bringing this up
- Okay, then from now on…

- I'm sure I don't remember as you do, but I am so sorry for how you have been thinking and feeling
- Look, what's important is that we want to move on
- I never intended it that way, but I see how you took it… I am truly sorry about how this has upset you

These promote a sense of relief that I finally told you, or they promote healing and enable people to move on. This is taking care of unfinished business.

C) The third kind of unfinished business is with people and events currently in your life. Because this person is such an ongoing part of your life, and the fact that something unfinished is getting in your way of feeling okay and getting in the way of the relationship, something needs to be done. This may require:

- a compliment
- an apology
- a request for forgiveness
- a reassurance of forgiveness
- an affirmation of pride, appreciation, and love
- an understanding that was never achieved
- an explanation
- a thank you
- a statement I have wanted to say or to hear

Sometimes efforts with someone else may prove to be ineffective and a sense of resolution does not get achieved. This happens because motivation, ability, and caring are lacking. We must find some ways to achieve peace on our own. At some point, it might be necessary to conclude, "There is nothing more I can do."

If the other is not available or willing to work with you, there are steps you can take to achieve peace.

1). Understanding. There may be factors that prevent the other person from being able to work with you. Lack of capability probably is easier to accept than unwillingness. Try to understand whatever the reality is.

2). Acceptance. After a reasonable amount of effort, there comes a time to say, "I've tried and I don't need to try again. It is now up to…" Once again, the mental health model that helps here is the Serenity Prayer. Learn it, understand it, internalize it, and live it.

3) Finally, let's be very clear about this unfinished business that gets dealt with healthily, but not happily. When the happy solution you're hoping for doesn't happen, you must settle for a sense of finishedness that doesn't necessarily feel good. It requires an intellectual strength of knowing you've done what you could and that's as good as it will get unless the other person changes and makes some efforts, which may be unlikely. Therefore, your task will be to accept what you can't change. When you think about it you will probably experience hurt, sadness, anger, or frustration, but this does not mean you're unhealthy or anything is wrong with you. What it means is you must handle a negative reality and not let it ruin your life. How can we do this?

- Self-discipline
- Distraction
- Sharing
- Turn it over

Self-Discipline

You must be willing and strong enough to stop yourself from getting caught in ruminating about the person or situation. This takes a tremendous amount of effort. However, in time it will get easier. If you allow yourself to mentally imagine a scenario with the other person or situation, it won't take long before you're stuck in emotions that accompany the moment as if it were actually happening. We are capable of making a thought feel as real as the actual event. If you go there, if you allow yourself to get caught in such thinking, you get stuck in the event. You can do this to yourself again and again. This is painful and brings back painful, negative feelings.

It is not "running from reality" to discipline yourself not to do this. You're preventing getting stuck in a reality that you really can't do anything about. You're not denying that this unfinished business exists; you're just not going to let yourself focus on it. This self-discipline will protect you. If you feel like it's too late to take this attitude, you've already developed an obsessive pattern of thinking about someone or something. Whatever the obsessive thought, give yourself permission to have time to obsess. Instead of obsessing throughout the day and at bedtime, set time aside to think about whatever the issue is, perhaps 2:00 – 2:30. Gradually shift from once a day to once a week. The goal is to delay the thoughts and eventually get over them. If you can't accomplish this on your own, seek professional help. This problem is very treatable. You don't need to suffer. If you work hard with someone, it will pay off.

Distraction

It's very difficult to just stop a thought or behavior and have no replacement, so, then what?" Create healthy distractions. Here are a few suggestions:

- Turn on music
- Call a friend
- Water the flowers
- Play with the kids
- Set a date to look forward to
- Say a prayer
- Pray for the other person

Positive distraction is a crucial step for mental and emotional wellness. Something to focus on, something to look forward to, these distractions protect you from getting stuck.

Sharing

Identify someone with whom you can periodically share your unfinished business with. You need someone with whom you can cry or release your frustrations and with whom you feel safe to describe the situation. Periodically having understanding support reduces the load of the unfinished business.

Also, knowing this person is out there helps you in your self-discipline to put it off until the two of you are together. This is a great idea. Use it prudently and moderately, but use it. Having such caring people in your life is a gift. As long as you don't abuse it by constant repeating, such friendships are what make the life journey joyful. Use it well.

Turn It Over

Laying it in the hands of your Higher Power may help you let go. Use your prayer life and meditation times to talk to God. "I've got to give this over to you. I don't know what more to do. Give me the strength to accept what I must accept." Jesus taught us by his own life that life can be unfair and relationships can let us down.

Exercise: Personal Unfinished Business

There are a number of ways to make personal assessment.

1) Personal Signs of Wellness
   - positive self-esteem – to think positively about oneself and to experience positive emotions
   - realistic thinking patterns about life and when it comes to expectations of oneself, of others and of life
   - a realistic and overall positive attitude about life
   - solid morals that are lived
   - solid values and priorities that keep life in perspective
   - self-discipline and impulse control – when necessary can "act differently than I feel" and think in terms of consequences
   - changes what can and should be, copes well with what can't be changed
   - a life characterized by emotional and behavioral consistency and predictability
   - a life with a sense of accomplishment, meaning, and purpose
   - gets along well with others; has adequate social skills; has meaningful and supportive relationships
   - handles and expresses emotions appropriately
   - has overall good communication skills: listens, understands, verbalizes, can be sensitive to what is being said. Sometimes might even hear what isn't being said
   - knows how to have fun – alone and with others and understands the importance of having things to look forward to
   - deals effectively with unfinished business – with oneself, as well as with others
   - no abuse or addictive patterns
   - capable of healthy intimacy
   - handles times well when things don't go our way

2) Review how you are doing with your six emotional needs. These needs are foundational for personal and interpersonal wellness. Review each one and question yourself how effectively and consistently you are meeting each.

3) Take a personal unfinished business inventory. Reflect on:
   - regrets: I wish I had… I wish I had not…
   - guilt's I struggle with…
   - anger, resentments I live with…
   - negative attitudes and beliefs I have that affect how I approach life
   - memories I sometimes or often struggle with…
   - do I have excessive mood swings, too-frequent ups and downs?

4) Reflect on your social skills and confidence. How are you doing with:
   - communication skills
   - impulse control
   - sexual attitudes and comfort
   - setting priorities
   - spirituality
   - handling money, alcohol, sex, food…

Be careful here. Realize that many of these behaviors and attitudes are probably sometimes true for most of us. Be aware if these behaviors occur more than "sometimes" in an unhealthy way. Many TV shows and movies depict personality disorders as the accepted norm. How does this affect you and your loved ones?

As you worked on the personal assessments earlier in this book, you probably thought of people who are part of your unfinished business, but at this point, just use these assessments to look only at yourself and the work you must do for your own growth. Truly identify what you need to do for your own well-being and health. You want to take charge of your own unfinished business so that it doesn't take charge of you and so it doesn't contaminate your relationships with others. Take time to make sure there is no significantly disturbing personal material that you must work on in order to be at peace with yourself and ready to move on in your relationships with others.

When I encourage you to take charge of what you need to do, I have two specific suggestions. Whichever one you choose should be determined by whether or not you can really do this work on your own or need someone else to help you. I personally believe most of us would do better with another person's help. However, you must honestly weigh this decision for yourself. If you try on your own and positive thoughts, feelings, behaviors, and patterns of living result, you did great. If you try and sense that you're still not where you need to be, then reach out for help.

After completing the various inventories and assessments, you can see what you need to do for yourself. Be very clear as to what you must accomplish regarding:

how I think
what my attitude is like
how free I am from old memories and experiences
what it means to be living effectively in the present and for the future
if I am making good, healthy, ethical decisions
how I feel; what emotions I live with
how stable my moods are
how I get along with others
my self-confidence and self-esteem
how my daily life goes
living the Serenity Prayer
honesty
sensitive to others, how I make others feel
my ability to act differently than I feel

Once you are clear on what you must do, find some solid self-help books. There are many excellent books currently available that can assist you in your personal work. Do some reading that leads you with exercises. A few I recommend are *Homecoming; I'm OK, You're OK* and *Born to Win*. These are old books, but wonderful. Some material is ageless! If, after making your own efforts, you sense you're still not where you need to be, then consider seeing a therapist, at least for a while. We can all benefit from talking with someone who can explore with us what needs to be seen and what needs to be done. We benefit from having someone who is sensitive to our feelings and helps us monitor our progress. My personal experiences, as a patient and as a therapist, have convinced me that there can be a tremendous benefit to having a professional relationship while working on our journey.

Exercise: Interpersonal Unfinished Business

1. Is there an issue from your past that continues to bring you feelings of unease? Explain the details you remember.

2. Does this event involve another person? Are they still part of your life? Do you sense that they care how this is affecting you, and are they likely to work on this with you?

3. How could you bring this up to them – a letter, a phone call, in person? Draft what you will say.

4. Does this issue involve someone who has already passed? Are you comfortable speaking to them in a spiritual way? Imagine the conversation you would have. Can you imagine reaching resolution and coming to a peaceful solution? What would you like to hear? Can you imagine them saying this to you?

5. If you cannot reach resolution with the person and you need to let it go, how can you use self-discipline to avoid rehashing the details?

6. What distractions can bring you joy and keep you from dwelling on unresolved unfinished business?

7. Who could help you process your thoughts and listen with understanding? Sharing can help you sort out your thoughts and consider other ideas you hadn't thought of.

8. Can you turn it over to a Higher Power? Take time for prayer and meditation. Write a prayer you can say when you feel old emotions surfacing.

Spiritual Reflection: Unfinished Business

Read each Scripture passage slowly. Pause between each passage for a couple of minutes. Take a few long gentle breaths. Close your eyes and try as best as you can to still your mind and let any words or phrases you just read cross your mind. Allow the thoughts to come and go. Sit and breathe slowly and gently with the thoughts as they come to you. If a word or phrase seems to stay with you, allow your mind to be still with that thought or phrase. Continue this process with each passage you chose to reflect upon.

- So then, if you bring your gift to the altar and there remember that your brother has something against you, leave your gift there in front of the altar. First go and be reconciled to your brother and then come and present your gift. (Matthew 5:23-24)

- If possible, so far as it depends on you, live peaceably with all people. (Romans 12:18)

- He did not waver in unbelief about the promise of God but was strengthened in faith, giving glory to God. He was fully convinced that what God promised he was also able to do. (Romans 4:20-21)

Reflection Questions:

Journal, discuss or silently reflect about the following questions:

1. Is there unfinished business with another person you would like to seek God's help to address? Pray about this and spend some time listening in prayer to God's response in your heart.

2. What spiritual practices can help keep you mindful of your unfinished business? (Such as meditating, spiritual direction, cultivating supportive friendships, etc.) How will you cultivate these practices in your life?

3. How can prayer help you with unfinished business with those who have died?

VI. FUN AND ANTICIPATION

Fun and Anticipation

It is uncomfortable leaving this need to the end of this section of the book because I am concerned people will regard it as the least important. It truly isn't. As a matter of fact, in some people's lives, it can be one of the most important emotional needs. The ability to have fun and the need to have something to look forward to are crucial.

This is also true when it comes to marriage and to family. The more they know how to play together, to have fun and laugh, the closer they will be. They are building relationships.

People who are suffering with depression often cannot name anything they are looking forward to. Huge problem!

We all need fun in our lives. We need to be able to look forward to enjoyable times. You should be able to make a list of things you have fun doing. These activities can be very different from accomplishments. Sometimes accomplishments aren't that much fun, though it is wonderful if you can combine the two and have fun while feeling a sense of accomplishment. That's why people who truly love their jobs are fortunate. They tend to be not only happy but also successful.

Can you think of activities you enjoy and look forward to? If you can't, then you probably need to look closely at the way you spend your time. Is your life all work and no play? You may need to cultivate some hobbies. Try tennis or gourmet cooking. Can you think of anything that you might enjoy? Scheduling fun and having something to look forward to can be as important as all the other work and personal tasks that make up your life.

There was a man in therapy who mentioned that his favorite pastime was playing the piano. When I asked him how long it had been since he had played, he said that it had been about four years ago when he was visiting his sister. This man was not allowing himself to do what he enjoyed most. When there is an activity that you really like, you should try to make it a regular part of your life. If you like to play bridge, join a bridge club. If you like the theater, consider buying season tickets. Whatever you like to do, work it into your life if at all possible.

Sometimes, circumstances may make it impossible to do what you would really like to do. Finances, health, time, and numerous other factors influence what we can and can't do. There are times when the demands of our lives handicap us and limit our options. This is a time to become creative and find ways to have fun within our limitations. This emotional need must be cared for, within whatever limitations exist. Having fun, alone and with others, is crucial to our mental, emotional, and physical well-being. Having fun things to look forward to is equally as important to our wellness. Think about how often having something to look forward to makes getting through a difficult time or a demanding time easier. We get some kind of energy knowing the fun or enjoyment will be coming.

You may have trouble with this need because of former truisms you learned. You might say, "First you work then you play." If this means to you that you must have *all* your work done before you play, you're in trouble. If you have a family, own a home or rent an apartment, or if you're active in your community, you're never finished with everything that needs to be done! If you want a new message, try "All work and no play make me a very dull person." It also makes you an unhealthy person.

You might be thinking, "A good person is someone who puts others' needs before their own." You should recognize that this kind of thought could cause you trouble. There needs to be balance. Guilt and unhealthy or unrealistic expectations of yourself can cripple your ability to enjoy yourself. What beliefs do you have that will *enhance* your ability to have fun or *interfere* with your ability to have fun? Identify them.

For example:

- If I don't get everything done, I'll be a terrible parent, homemaker, spouse, daughter…
- If I think of myself, I'm selfish
- I am entitled to have good times. These rejuvenate me

Make a commitment to yourself to, *"act differently than I feel"*. It is crucial. You know that self-discipline is a big part of successful therapy. Discipline yourself to putting things to look forward to on your weekly/monthly schedule. If money is an issue, think of creative things to do at home or with friends at each other's home. Rent a film versus going to the movies. Have friends over and everyone bring something, including their own beverages. Instead of paying for a babysitter, arrange with another couple to swap nights out and alternate babysitting for one another. Lots of creative ideas are possible.

It is easier to get through the difficult parts of life when we have something to anticipate – a Friday night fish fry, a vacation, a good book to read, an exciting movie, a workout, a card game, or lunch with someone. Think of activities you could plan that would energize you because you can look forward to them.

Another important question to ask yourself is, "Can I have fun with another person, particularly my spouse or another significant person?" Most married people need to have some fun activity they look forward to together. If you can't have fun with each other, then how enjoyable is it to be part of such a relationship? Relationships need pleasurable times. If a couple doesn't have fun together, doesn't look forward to good times, what incentives are there for making up? The ability to enjoy good times and to anticipate them are ingredients that motivate people to get the negatives out of the way. They know that as long as negative feelings are there, they will be missing out on good times. What must you do to get the fun back?

Having fun together is also important to the parent and child relationship. Parents sometimes comment that they wish their children would talk with them about the important matters in their lives. These parents need to think about the times they and their children have fun together. When a child of any age feels comfortable with someone, that child is more likely to share his or her feelings, thoughts, questions, and concerns.

Think about the people who are close to you. Is having fun together one of the factors that brought you together? Do you share yourself and your problems with people who are not your friends? Spend some time thinking about this, and talk with your close friends and relatives about your awareness. Share with them what you would like to do together for fun, for enjoyment.

In a society that emphasizes acting the way you feel - "if it feels good, do it," knowing how to balance responsibility and play is an interesting and difficult challenge. Equally as concerning is how our sense of morality and values has been jaded by what our society encourages. So many mistakes are being made by people making decisions based upon what feels good. If, to have fun, people get hurt, you abuse drugs and alcohol, and disregard values, then you risk your own and others' safety. These decisions are unhealthy and are not what I mean when I encourage meeting the needs for fun and anticipation.

If you are unable to play, to have fun, and to have things to look forward to, address and work to change this. Often times, this problem happens because of self-esteem problems or some unfinished business issue. Whatever the cause that interferes with adequately caring for this emotional need, make a commitment to yourself and with significant others to correct what's wrong. Be creative; be willing to push yourself. Work on an attitude that enables you to be playful and fun. Keep this need an important one in your life and in your relationship with others.

Exercise: Fun and Anticipation

Set some time aside right now to think about the following.

1. What do you have fun doing? Make a list here.

2. When was the last time you did each one? How often do you make them part of your life? How many of the activities on your list can you do alone versus needing someone else to enjoy it with?

3. When I think about my daily and weekly schedule, where is time for myself? Where is time for me and someone I enjoy to have fun together? Readjusting one's schedule is a huge challenge for wellness!

4. If I recognize my schedule needs to be adjusted, where will I specifically carve out the personal and interpersonal time I need? Will I be able to stay committed? Will we stay committed?

5. Pick up the list of fun activities that I encouraged you to make earlier. Remember, you don't always need to be active to have fun. Is your list extensive enough? Should you come up with more ideas?

6. Now think of some significant others and list specific activities to do and look forward to with each of them. Think about what you would enjoy doing together.

7. Think about your life for the next couple of days, weeks, and months. What will you be doing? What is happening and being expected of you? Would it help to accomplish what you need to and feel better about pushing yourself through these expectations or situations if you had something to look forward to? In a sense, this is like having a reward at the end of a task. What do you think about this? What would such planning ahead do for your energy and for your mood?

The goal for each of us is a balanced life which includes meeting our personal, interpersonal, and professional responsibilities, while also experiencing the fun and pleasures we like. As with the other five emotional needs, this is an essential task for your well-being, and it will require your commitment to work at it. Don't minimize this need. Between selfishness and self-denial there is a healthy middle ground. Find this for yourself and in your relationships with others.

Spiritual Reflection: Fun and Anticipation:

Read each Scripture passage slowly. Pause between each passage for a couple of minutes. Take a few long gentle breaths. Close your eyes and try as best as you can to still your mind and let any words or phrases you just read cross your mind. Allow the thoughts to come and go. Sit and breathe slowly and gently with the thoughts as they come to you. If a word or phrase seems to stay with you, allow your mind to be still with that thought or phrase. Continue this process with each passage you chose to reflect upon.

- Therefore my heart is glad and my tongue rejoices; my body also will live in hope. (Acts 2:26)

- These things I have spoken to you, that my joy may remain in you, and that your joy may be full. (John 14: 11)

- Then he said to them, "Go your way, eat the fat, drink the sweet, and send portions to those for whom nothing is prepared; for this day is holy to our Lord. Do not sorrow, for the joy of the Lord is your strength." (Nehemiah 8:10)

- When times are good, be happy; but when times are bad, consider: God has made the one as well as the other. (Ecclesiastes 7:14)

Reflection Questions:

Journal, discuss or silently reflect about the following questions:

1. Do you think there is a difference between fun and joy? How do you cultivate experiences of fun and anticipation? How do you cultivate joy?

2. What is the difference between pleasure and happiness? What gives you pleasure? What brings you happiness?

3. How do you find the balance between living in the moment and anticipation of the future?

4. How is being able to look forward to spending time with _______ a joyful anticipation?

Review Exercise: Six Emotional Needs

1. Can you name the six emotional needs?

2. Evaluate how satisfied you are with how well each need is being met in your life – by your own efforts or by your efforts with someone else.
   A. Is the need being met healthily and consistently?
   B. If the need is going unmet, if you are hurting because of what is or is not happening, create a plan to improve the situation.

I. Sense of Security

1. What changes must you make? Do you need to have a calendar, with regularly scheduled activities?

2. Are there certain people or situations where you need them to be more reliable, consistent, predictable, and trustworthy?

3. Are there people and relationships or situations like employment, health, or finances, where you have tried to do all you can and now you must learn to cope with what you can't change?
   - Change what I can…
   - Expect others to change what they can…
   - Cope effectively with what I can't change …
   - Develop coping skills like prayer, healthy attitude, exercise, people to talk with
   - Write your own gratitude list and read it regularly

4. Where or with whom do you find yourself "walking on eggshells," where you are often nervous about what will happen next? What can be done about it? Who should you turn to? Find out if the person cares about how you feel. Discuss what should be done differently so that this "eggshell" feeling doesn't happen. Create a concise agreement that you both want to be more comfortable around each other and agree on what will be different from now on. For example: a change in voice tone, attitude, responding when appropriate, taking responsibility for initiating a conversation, and certain behavioral changes that affect you.

5. What changes do others need you to make?

6. Is trusting an issue? If so, why? About what? What do you need to know and be able to count on?

7. Is someone having trouble trusting you? What are you doing about this? What does someone else need you to do?

II. Sense of Accomplishment, Purpose, and Meaning

1. What are you doing on a regular basis to feel a sense of purpose, meaning, and accomplishment?

2. Are you personally committed to keeping that activity going?

3. Are significant others supporting you and encouraging you in this area of your life?

4. Are you willing to search for meaningful activities? Are you willing to make yourself act differently than you feel and try new things? Volunteer, call somebody else to do something new with you, take a class… get creative.

5. Ask someone to write an ad for you, highlighting your skills, achievements, abilities, and potential. You aren't ignoring flaws or negatives – you're just not going to talk about them in the ad. Your friend knows that. The point is that you just want to hear about and be able to focus on the positives and what they see you accomplishing in life and what you're good at.

6. If you have trouble making a positive checklist about yourself, why not work with someone – a professional or a friend – to help you list your accomplishments? What meaningful, purposeful things do they see you doing in your life? Which ones should you learn to do?

III. Positive Self-Esteem

1. Write an ad for the newspaper describing yourself.

2. Did you write the ad like a job application or a dating application?

3. Read your ad to yourself. How does it make you feel? On a scale of 1 – 10, how much self-esteem does your ad reflect? If pleased, know why and take comfort in this. If displeased, what can you do about it? Are you failing to appreciate what is wonderful about you?

If there were negative experiences and messages in your past, it is time to erase these "tapes" and begin to replace them with new messages and beliefs. Developing appreciative, positive, and loving thoughts and beliefs about yourself can definitely be done. As you develop these thoughts and beliefs, you will also start to experience the corresponding positive feelings. Whatever the past personal or interpersonal regrets, remember, "God doesn't create junk." You are special and should work to believe this!

Whatever happened or didn't happen, whatever personal regrets and shame, whatever traumatic event along the journey, must this baggage continue to be in your "backpack of daily living?" It's time to forgive yourself. It's time to challenge any past event that you are letting hurt your self-esteem. It's time to approach each day with new, positive, affirming messages in your head. It's time to look in the mirror and tell that person to love themself. It's time to go to the book store and get a meditation book that focuses on self-worth. It may be time to work with someone about appreciating and valuing yourself. Whatever the yesterdays, todays, and tomorrows, love and value yourself! What must you think and believe to accomplish this?

IV. Relationships

1. Do you have people in your life who are important to you and who consider you important to them? Who are they?

2. What makes them so wonderful and valuable to you?

3. Have you told them about their importance?

4. How would you go about doing so? Make a commitment to do so – in person, on the phone, or in writing. Think about what you would say. Write a draft first, even if you plan to talk to them in person.

5. How does it feel to imagine sharing like this? Turn it around – how would you feel if this person shared a letter of appreciation written to you? Should you let them know how much you would appreciate one?

6. So, what are you going to commit to do? With whom? How? By when? Anyone that goes back years?

V. Unfinished Business – Personal and Interpersonal

1. Is anything from your past interfering with your peace?
2. Do any of the following seem to bother you a great deal?
   - Regrets that I did…. or didn't …
   - Guilt over some choice(s) you made
   - Anger regarding…
   - That when you think of __________, you become upset
   - That there is something from the past that feels unresolved
   - That makes you sad
   - That I have told ____ …

3. The power of this emotional need is that, whether with yourself or with someone else or with some event of your life, you must find some ways to end being weighed down. You should not be caught in memories, emotions, and thoughts that interfere with your ability to live effectively in the present. If you were going to draw a picture of how this need would look if unfinished business existed, it might look like you are trying to walk down the road of life but there is a rope around you with an anchor stuck in the road. Or huge boulders in the way prevent you from moving forward.

Draw this picture, or one similar to it, and identify any anchors or boulders that make it difficult for you to live in the present and move forward. Label the anchors or boulders giving them some specific identity. What do you see? Who do you see? What does the picture tell you that you need to do? Do you have unfinished business? If so, let's see how the following exercises can help you.

Managing Personal Unfinished Business

1. If some guilt, regret, disappointment, frustration, embarrassment, shame, or unfulfilled experience is powerful in your life, write it down.

2. Look at what you wrote. What do you think about when you look at it? Write your thoughts. For example, "When I think about ___, I begin to think ___." Whether you are writing or thinking, become aware of how your thoughts result in certain emotions. "When I think about ___, I end up feeling ___." What do you need to depower? What new beliefs and attitudes must you work at?

3. What are my attitudes and beliefs about being an imperfect person?

4. What does it mean:
    - to forgive?
    - to forgive myself?
    - to learn from my past?
    - to grow from my past?
    - to accept that "it is done" or "it is too late"?
    - to admit and accept that "at the time I did what I did?"
    - to admit and accept that I made a terrible mistake?
    - to admit and accept that "if I could do it over I would… or I wouldn't …"?

Notice how important it is *to admit* and *to accept.* Remember the power of the philosophy "change what I can and cope with what I can't change."

Managing Interpersonal Unfinished Business

With whom in your life do you feel unfinished, unresolved, not at peace?

- Who is this?
- What is the unresolved, painful, unsettling issue? What happened? What didn't happen?
- How long has it been an issue?
- What specific feelings does it stir up?
- What consequences has this person or event had for you?
- What have you tried to do about it?
- What would you like to do about it?
- Have you tried enough and it's time to stop trying?
- Is there something you want and need to say to someone?
- What are you going to do about it?

An exercise that can be very helpful is to write the person a letter. Even if the person has passed away, this writing can still be helpful. Realize that you can say everything you need to say. Then, if you want, rip up the letter. Just get everything out of you that needs to come out.

Sometimes it may be better not to bring up something to a person who has caused us pain. This confrontation needs to be sensitively thought through. There is a big difference between healing and growing with someone versus passing the pain onto them in order to free yourself. This is a very difficult issue. I would suggest that if you are struggling with an issue like this in your life, you process it and look at what to do with a neutral party like a pastor, therapist, or trusted friend. The bottom line is that you find some effective way to reach some level of inner peace. Know what you need to do. Don't ignore this important work.

VI. Fun and Anticipation

1. Check in on your ability to have regularly scheduled good times in your life, alone and with others, and to have things to look forward to.

    - What do you have fun doing?

    - When was the last time you did it?

    - Have you made plans to do so?

    - Are your fun times by yourself or with others?

    - Do you have fun often enough? If not why not?

    - Do you overdo fun in your life at the expense of someone or something? What is this about?

    - Do you and some significant others need to commit to having more fun more often?

    - What would it do for your mood to have things to look forward to?

    - Will this need require you to make yourself act and do differently than you feel?

Final Encouragement

1. After completing these many questions about you and your life, what do you realize you need to do? Is your work all personal work? How much in your own life needs to be changed, revisited, and healed? How much work requires you and someone else?

2. Are you able to do this personal or interpersonal work on your own, or is some professional intervention needed? I know it can be uncomfortable, even scary, to answer this last question honestly. Please think it through carefully because you can accomplish so much for yourself and with significant others if you put energy into working with a professional.

3. After all is said and done, whatever you decide you need to do for yourself and your relationships, commit to the crucial task of taking care of these six emotional needs. I hope this first chapter has helped you to begin heal, to grow, to be more at peace, and to experience joy within yourself and with others.

SPIRITUALITY OF THE PERSON

It's All about Relationships

It doesn't matter if you are reading a current magazine, the latest book on business theory, the current thinking in quantum physics or the Bible… you are bound to get the message, relationships are pretty important to us. We human beings seem to be simply wired for relationships. Margaret Wheatley, author and organizational management leader said, "Relationship is the key determiner of everything" (Wheatley, 2006). "Relationships are all there is" (Wheatley, 2002).

It appears we are intrinsically wired for "relationships to be everything". And with relationships come the agony and the ecstasy of human interaction. The ancient stories recorded in the Sacred Scriptures continue to provide inspiration and relevance today because they are basically about relationships, between humanity with the divine and between human persons. With relationships come… culture and diversity and the need to relate, accommodate and understand. Relationships cause us to engage in attachment, loyalty, jealousy, conflict and call us to cultivate higher virtues such as, sacrifice, service, respect, compassion and care. Hence, a science is born to learn how to negotiate relationships.

> For as long as we have been around as humans, as wandering bands of nomads or cave dwellers, we have sat together and shared experiences. We have painted pictures on rock walls, recounted dreams and visions, told stories of the day, and generally felt comforted to be in the world together. When the world became fearsome, we came together. When the world called us to explore its edges, we journeyed together. Whatever we did we did it together.
>
> (Margaret Wheatley, Turning to One Another: Simple Conversations to Restore Hope to the Future, 2002, p. 4)

Relationships are everything because we need each other. Is it because the human species is biologically wired that way and or our brains have adjusted our behavior to such a high social and emotional intelligence as to create a relational culture? Or is it because God created that plan and relating is the purpose for God's beloved human creatures? Whatever your beliefs, here we are mattering to each other, needing each other, having gifts to give each other, continually learning how to get along with each other. We do not know God's mind but we move closer to the person God intends us to be when we realize how much we have to give each other. Maturity leads us to insights about our relationships, such as, we are enhanced by appreciation of diversity and we get along better when we have sensitivity to another's culture and reasonable minds can differ. Relationships simply go better in a context of respect, compassion and care and within a willingness to be of service to each other.

It is a choice in life to deliberately focus to see our relationships as a *sacred* opportunity. Some religious perspectives would express that relationships are our opportunity to work out salvation in life. Some would say each day, every interaction, gives us the opportunity to have an impact on the lives of others. Many find truth and meaning in the saying, "Life is God's gift to you. What you do with that life is your gift to God."

Do you recognize the gifts God has uniquely given you? Do you realize, wonder and ponder the truth that there is only one you? Our relationships are the chance to use our gifts to enhance the lives of others, those in our family, our work environment, our community.

The Unique Gift <u>You</u> Have To Give!

No one else ever created will have your unique talents, opportunities, gifts, perspectives and even the weaknesses and limitations that make you uniquely you. Missing the importance of this thought, this one fact, could deprive the world of what you singularly and uniquely have to contribute. There will be words of love unspoken, acts of courage not performed, hurts not healed, hope not offered, tender touch not given, the great idea not contributed, if we do not realize who we are, what we have to give and how very much we matter!

Living each day with awareness of this can be the core of understanding of what it means to live deeply and spiritually. Transcending beyond knowledge of any doctrinal truth or religious affiliation means above all else that we *respect life*... beginning with the life you have been given. Your one life and how you live it will affect the course of events in the world. You are a unique being, a onetime gift from the Divine Creator to the human race. You have the power to decide what to do with that gift of your life. The poet Mary Oliver, asks in her poem, "A Summer Day", the important question: "Tell me, what is it you plan to do with your one wild and precious life?" (Mary Oliver, *New and Selected Poems*)

History has given us great and deplorable examples of what can be done with that gift of life. A simple Albanian born woman became one of the great inspirations of contemporary history by choosing to love the poorest of the poor as embodied in the person of Blessed Mother Teresa of Calcutta. The wealthy child of an upper class Italian family became the great advocate of simplicity and peace, St. Francis of Assisi. These witnesses to spiritual greatness are a gift as exemplars of the power of life focused on higher values. In fact, a sign of significant spiritual development is to come to love what God loves: the poor, the vulnerable and to espouse the values Scripture would indicate that God treasures: peace, justice, compassion and forgiveness.

Unfortunately, history has also witnessed selfishness and cruelty in political dictators and evildoers who decided to use their gifts to wreak havoc in the world. You in your own personal and private life have probably experienced once or countless times the power of how unconditional love gave beauty and meaning to your life. You may personally have also experienced the devastation of someone making a choice to act or speak in such a way that wounded or hurt you in some profound way. Forgiving and moving on from such hurt in our own life is an act of love and, though possibly very difficult, shows great courage.

Have you been given the sacred responsibility to love another person? A child? A spouse? A parent? A friend? Had it occurred to you the potential you have in that relationship? I recently read a memoir in which the author told of harboring something said to her, a one sentence remark that her spouse spoke to her about her body. As I read the story of her life I was in awe that it took years to reveal the impact those words had on her emotional life. When she did tell her husband, he apologized and in the narrative, explained his remark. His intention was not malicious but held a very benign meaning in his mind. It was almost painful to read the story and feel the torment the woman experienced for years from the power of a thoughtless remark and it was inspiring to imagine the power to heal that occurred in one courageous conversation between the two persons.

Harnessing the Power of God's Presence in You

When I was in high school I was involved in a volunteer role at my church. I taught a religious education class to a group of young children. The woman in charge of the program wrote a card to me at the end of the year thanking me for teaching. She said in the note, "Whatever the question, you, Kathie, will answer it with love." I cannot express the power of that one sentence in my self-image. I don't know why she chose those particular words but I have often wondered over the years if I deserved them as a reflection of what she saw me as or if she was giving me an ideal to live up to. Either way was a gift. I can never thank her enough for that. Though I have made many many mistakes and undoubtedly have fallen short of living up to her aspiration for me countless times, her words have been a compass through these many years. We don't know what the questions of our life are going to be but the spiritual path for the one who wishes to be a follower of Christ is to answer them with love. Jesus answered the questions in his life with love over and over again as we learn from Scripture.

You may ask, "So what is spiritual about this story of one sentence someone wrote to me that took root in my heart?" I would answer, "Inside this little story is a precious concept. It is that you can wake up each day and trust that you have the power to use every thought, word and act of that day to create goodness and life in your relationships. God gives you the day. What you do with the moments of your day is your gift back to God." To live each day with focused sustained awareness of the importance of what we say and how we act in our relationships is to live in a spiritually rich and enriching way. Intentionally, practicing this *awareness* will change the course, the direction and the meaning of your life.

So how do we do that? Here are a few ideas. One, begin the day with a thought, a prayer, a brief meditation, inviting awareness of the potential of your words and actions of that day. Many religious traditions have versions of specific *morning prayer*. In other words, begin your day with some words of inspiration to direct your thoughts and actions that day. This may work even better if you consider beginning your day with a short mantra rather than a long prayer or ritual. A few are suggested below. It may take some time to develop this habit.

Mantras

"God, be my strength today"

"In your honor"

"Teach me to love today"

"Make my life a prayer today"

"Grant me peace"

"Give me what I need today to live a full, abundant and generous life"

"My life is in your hands, O Lord"

"The LORD is my shepherd, I shall not be in want" (Psalm 23)

"I can do all things through Christ who strengthens me" (Philippians 4:13)

"Love is patient, love is kind" (1 Corinthians 13:4)

"Trust in the Lord with all your heart" (Proverbs 3:5)

One suggestion is to allow a little more time between waking and rising. Sometimes the gentle entry into the day reminds us to be gentle with ourselves as well as others. You may find it helpful to allow a little more time between waking up and getting up. Giving the day a reflective and gentle start, to gradually and simply train your first thoughts to be awareness of your own breathing and review of your dreams or waking thoughts begins the day more calmly than rushing from awakening from sleep to a flurry of preparatory activity getting ready for the day. Take the time to wake gently. Thank God for the new day. Give thanks for the waking and another day of life. Consider how you would wake a beloved child. Wouldn't we warmly greet them with happy words and affectionate gestures? What affect would it have on your day to treat yourself with such gentleness?

Did you give yourself breath this morning? Or was it a gift? If you believe it a gift, give thanks to the power who gave it to you. *Gratitude* is a way of life that primes us for the understanding that relationships begin not with us, but with the life force that sustains us. In the Christian tradition we call that Creator, God. God begins the relationship with us from our conception and birth and renews it each day in the first breath of the morning.

Second, as your day begins, put some little reminder of the opportunities to see the sacred presence of God that are presented to you this day. Place a religious statue or spiritual image of something sacred to you near your nightstand or on the sink where you will brush your teeth. Have a picture of a loved one, a child, a parent, a friend, living or deceased, where you will see the picture upon waking. Let that be a reminder of your potential to be loving, peaceful and kind in your words and actions on this day that will only be given to you once in this lifetime! Think of how you would treat the loved one who is imaged in the picture. Promise yourself to treat everyone, in each of your relationships, the way you would treat that pictured loved one. Ask God's blessings on this day. Viewing each day as an opportunity to love others is to make that day, *a sacred day*.

As you move through your day try to remember to think before you speak to others. Do your responses to others lift them up? In

Paul's letter to the Ephesians, he invites us to consider our words as gifts wrapped in silver boxes.

> *Let no unwholesome word proceed from your mouth,*
> *but only such a word as is good for edification*
> *according to the need of the moment, so that it will give*
> *grace to those who hear. (Ephesians 4:29)*

Are your words chosen to encourage those around you to feel appreciated, respected, significant? If you find yourself complaining, nagging, discouraging... stop. Take a breath. Silently try to stay aware of your breathing until you are able to remind yourself of the importance of your words and actions and how they will affect others. Pull out that morning mantra as needed throughout the day. Use that inner mantra to center yourself in what is really important to you... who you are becoming as a person. Try through a simple consistent thought to remind yourself, "Relationships are everything" or "Grant me peace" or "Teach me love" or "My life is in your hands, O Lord." Or think of something, in a simple way, you find helpful to remind you of the sacred responsibility of your life and the potential you have to improve the lives of those around you.

When I was a child in Catholic grade school we were instructed to write on the top of each paper of our schoolwork, the initials, *JMJ*, to remind us to ask Jesus, Mary and Joseph to be with us, spiritually, as we worked on that particular assignment. Such practices are not usually done today. But they were a tangible reminder of the spiritual opportunity in the ordinary tasks of life. You might find reviving the spirit of such practices helpful, such as saying a silent quick prayer, such as, *God be with me,* before composing an email, or taking that slow deep breath before speaking, to remind you to be respectful to others in your speech.

I have also found the use of a sacred object to be helpful in centering myself in my spiritual values. I wear a medal on a chain that was given to me by a friend as a keepsake from a spiritual place in my faith tradition. When I touch the medal hanging daily from my neck I am reminded of this sacred place, and of the miracle it commemorates that we believed was experienced there and also that I have a friend who loved me enough to share the spiritual gift with me. It has allowed me to find my spiritual center in challenging moments and through difficult conversations to help me remember who I want to be and that I and everyone around me is a precious child of God and to try to act accordingly.

The Spirituality of the Pause

Busyness is the crisis of our present culture. Even children and retired persons are routinely heard to comment on being overly busy and stressed by the pace of life. Technology has brought many wonderful opportunities to us as human beings but if it encourages a pace of busyness, of living life that does not allow for appreciation and joy in life we are misusing the gift. Sometime during each day… pause. Simply pause at your desk, your kitchen sink, looking into the eyes of your spouse or your child and whisper a slow sincere, *thank you,* for the gift of the moment. How would life change for you if you did that once a day, five times a day, fifty times a day? Such a spiritual practice would take less than a minute out of the day but might change the quality of the busy lives we lead.

The Expiration Date

Relationships are the way we are wired as human beings to live in social cultures. To live spiritually is to live in awareness and consciousness of the great opportunity of the gift of our life. A splendid gift! A divine gift! It is not morbid, but is motivating, to realize this is a great gift but we all have *an expiration date* on the gift of our life. Everything I have and am, aside from my soul, will pass away, it will not last forever. The physical gifts of mobility, intellect, hearing, sight, and the strength to relate, to contribute, to share, to dance, to dream, will not last forever. To live in the spiritual awareness of this can inspire us to appreciate what we do have and not to keep the time we are given in life for granted. As you go about your day, consider what a difference it would make to intentionally affirm, encourage and appreciate others. Just think, *how you could offer, a word of hope or consolation or appreciation to another person that would make a difference in their lives!*

A friend, who had recently lost her ninety-year-old father, shared a tearful and loving memory of her Dad. As elderly and frail as he grew, he insisted upon getting up from his recliner with the help of a motorized lift each time they parted from a visit. When she said "Dad, don't get up." He said, "No, I have to." And he slowly, gently, but with great effort, rose to his feet and opened his arms and hugged her. She shared the memory as if she was opening her palms showing me a rare flower. What a gift a simple embrace can be. This was a gift she would treasure for the rest of her life. Even his death could not diminish the preciousness or spiritual power of this memory for her.

What a tragedy for a father, a mother, a child, a friend, not to recognize this precious gift that we each have to give! What a loss to miss that hug we can give each other! What a shame to not appreciate the potential we each have to change the world by recognizing the gifts we have to bestow on each other! It is so easy to take life and others in our life for granted. We have so many simple gifts for each other! Our care and affection may not be given because we neglect the opportunity of the moment, or lack appreciation of the power we have to heal and edify another. These small decisions often make up the quality of our life and of those around us. The spiritual richness of our life can be enhanced by these relational gifts given. The poet, Emily Dickinson advised, that we "dwell in possibility". What good advice!

Chapter Two

BUILDING A HEALTHY COUPLE RELATIONSHIP

Building a Healthy Couple Relationship

I – take you – to be my spouse.
To have you in my life. To hold you. To care for you.
To travel the life journey with you.
I will be there for you, in good times and in bad;
in sickness and in health; during joyful times and unhappy times;
when life seems easy and when it is difficult.
I make this vow to you and I promise to live up to this vow.

For many of you, this vow probably has some familiarity. You can remember pledging such a vow or are preparing one for your future marriage. What is a vow? It is a promise, a statement of commitment. In this particular example, it is the promise to work as a partner on making the marriage a healthy, satisfying, and effective relationship. When two mature people make the marriage vow, they are promising to be there for one another during all sorts of life's moments. The couple knows that there will be challenging, unhappy, disappointing times. There will be times when you will not feel in love. There will be times when asking "if you're glad you married me" may not be a really good question.

We live in a society that places so much emphasis on how we feel – "if it feels good it must be right; and if it feels bad, it must be wrong." These are terribly wrong beliefs to have about marriage. Solid, healthy, satisfying, effective marriages will at times not feel so wonderful. However, healthy couples, those committed-to-their-vow, realize moments like these will happen, but they work through them. They realize that this relationship will take work and that, in addition to the wonderful, easy times, there will be times requiring effort and the willingness to be sorry, to forgive, to change, and to grow. These two people must not only be verbally committed to the efforts as a couple, they must also be personally ready to do so.

What does this mean? When you think of anything you do in life, you recognize that if you want to do it well and be competent, you must personally prepare yourself. You must think about it, learn about it, and practice it. You must be personally ready to succeed at it. So too when it comes to marriage. Am I ready? Are we ready? Or, another way to ask this – "Are each of us old enough to be married?"

Consider this quote:

> *The individual who has not learned to be happy as a single person has just as little chance of being happy in marriage. Marriage can never be an escape from responsibility into which infantile adults can flee from self-development. A marriage partner is not to be recruited as a babysitter for an infantile adult.*
>
> *(Marriage for the Millions)*

The powerful message in this quote is that it emphasizes that the first ingredient for a successful marriage is two relatively healthy individuals. Each must be "ready" for the challenge of marriage. Each must be "old enough" to be married."

Let me tell you where this "old enough to be married" comes from. Around 1990, I was seeing a young couple who had three children, ages 8, 7, and 4. The eight-year-old and the four-year-old were girls. Sammy was the seven-year-old brother. Mom and Dad had been in treatment for a number of weeks and it was time to have the children meet me. "Who is this Dr. Meske Mom and Dad were seeing?" It was a pretty common practice to make sure the children had some idea about who I was, where Mom and Dad were coming, and to let them know that, if ever they needed to talk to someone or to understand something, they could call me.

Therefore, I had the three kids come in to see me. After some brief talking, I asked the kids why they think Mommy and Daddy were coming in to see me. They often know that it's because their parents aren't happy with each other; that they aren't getting along. What I do to help the kids understand what is going on and what their parents are going through is to tell them the story of the *Bird and the Fish*, a book I wrote for parents and children going through divorce.

I tell the story about a bird and fish who could be wonderful friends. The bird could drop worms in the water for the fish to eat and the fish could throw seaweed out on the shore for the bird to build a nest. They could even play catch with one another. Then I ask them, what would happen if one of them, the bird or fish, went to live with the other? The children know that if the bird tried to live under water or the fish tried to live in the nest, one of them would die. I then point out that their mom and dad are working with me to figure out if they are two birds or two fishes that could learn to live with one another or if they are a bird and a fish that, although they are able to be wonderful friends, they cannot live together. Children find this to be a very understandable story.

Then I tell the children that, while I'm working with their parents, if they are ever upset about something or need to talk with me about anything, they can give me a phone call. I give each of them my card and write my cell phone and clinic numbers on the back. I tell them to put their cards on their dresser in their room and, if ever they need to, they can call me.

Well, one day while playing golf, I received a phone call from the answering service.

"Dr. Meske, Sammy is on the phone."

"Sammy? Are you sure it's Sammy? He's only 7-years-old."

"Yes, Dr. Meske, the little boy said he was Sammy, and he's crying."

"Hi Sammy; this is Dr. Meske. What can I do for you?"

"Dr. Meske, it's horrible here. Mommy and Daddy are fighting again. They're yelling at each other. My sisters and I don't know what to do. We are afraid."

"Sammy, where are your two sisters?"

"They're right here next to me."

"Well, listen, Sammy. I'm really glad you called me. Go tell your mommy and daddy that I'm on the phone and ask them if they will bring the three of you to my office tomorrow after school."

"They said we could come in at 3:00pm."

"OK, great. I'll see you tomorrow at 3:00pm. Are you and your sisters going to be okay until then?"

"Yes."

"Great. Ask your sisters if either of them want to say anything or ask me anything."

"No, they don't want to talk now."

"OK, Sammy. We're all set for tomorrow. Sammy, do you see my phone number on the back of the card?"

"Yes, Dr. Meske."

"Well, if you or your sisters need to call me later, you can call me at the home phone. Do you understand this?"

"Yes, Dr. Meske."

"OK, see you tomorrow."

The next day at 3:00pm, the three kids were in my office. I pulled a chair up close to the three of them and told them I was very glad they called me and I was surely pleased that we were now able to get together. Each of them looked sad and tired. Sammy had on his baseball cap, pulled to the side. If you were going to pick a boy to play Huckleberry Finn, Sammy would be your choice.

I asked them to tell me what all goes on at home. What do they hear? What do they see or imagine happening? How does it make them feel? I mentioned that it must be scary to be around them when they act like this. I bet it makes them very scared. They all nodded their heads. At one point I asked, "Well what do you think is going on with your mommy and daddy? Why do they act this way?" After a short pause, Sammy looked up and said:

"You know, Dr. Meske, I don't think they're old enough to be married."

Well, my heart leapt into my throat and I felt the tears welling up in my eyes. I looked at the three of them and said, "Sammy, you are so right. Sometimes, mommies and daddies don't act old enough to be married."

I thought that it was very important to affirm Sammy, to let him and his sisters know that what they were hearing and seeing were not the way things were supposed to go on between two adults. I believed it was important not to defend or to excuse their parents' behavior. I did not want to confuse the three kids about what was appropriate and what was not. Sammy, with the wisdom and blunt innocence of a child, had said something very powerful, insightful, and truthful. Sammy and his sisters needed to know that I agreed with them. And, their parents needed to know about this wonderful insight and how I affirmed it with their children.

I have told this story to hundreds of couples. Think about how significant Sammy's statement is: "old enough to be married." What does this mean to a child? "Old enough" means to be ready for, able to do. "I am old enough to ride my bike, stay up late, sleep in my own bed, etc. Old enough means I am ready for this next step in life."

So then what does it mean to be old enough to be married? It means being ready for marriage. It means knowing what you need to know and being personally able and willing to live it. It means that if you find out that something isn't working right between the two of you, you admit it and live up to your vow to learn what you need to learn and then work at it together. In so very many ways, we find out so much about ourselves and each other and marriage after we're married. Therefore, once we discover the demands of marriage, we better be "old enough" to work at it!

To explore the many ingredients necessary for a healthy, satisfying, effective marriage, we must start with the first ingredient – that the relationship be made up by two healthy individuals who are personally ready and "old enough" for marriage.

First ingredient – A Healthy, "Old Enough to be Married" Person

When thinking about what it means to be personally healthy and ready, let's look at four criteria to examine within yourself and about your partner:

1. Effectively taking care of the six emotional needs
2. An understanding of personal history and life experiences that have influenced who you are, how you think, feel, react, and behave.
3. Recognizing what you are or are not capable of. Am I someone who can…? who will not…?
4. The absence of clinical concerns.

1) Our Six Emotional Needs

The six emotional needs was the material in the first chapter of this book. Quick review:

1) <u>Sense of Security</u>

   This means that you are someone who is predictable, consistent, reliable, trustworthy, and you do not cause others to "walk on eggshells". It also means life has got some predictability to it; there's consistency both in your own life and with others.

2) Sense of Accomplishment
   You have a sense of accomplishment and meaning/purpose in your life; you take pride in yourself.
3) Positive Self Esteem
   You think positively about yourself and regard yourself as likable, loveable, worthwhile, and capable. You expect to be treated with respect. Keep in mind that, although all the emotional needs are crucial, positive self-esteem is certainly the most crucial because it is foundational.
4) Satisfying Relationships
   You have people in your life to whom you are very important and who are very important to you.
5) No Unfinished Business
   Whether within yourself or in your relationships with others, you have done what you needed to in order to find resolution within yourself or with others.
6) Fun and Anticipation
   You regularly have fun in your life and have events you look forward to.

The first inventory to take to help you determine if you are personally healthy and ready for marriage is how effectively you and your partner are taking care of these emotional needs - on your own, with each other, and with others.

2) Self Knowledge

Who or what has played a role and influenced the person you are? If you were to watch the "(Your name) Story" what would that movie look like from birth until today? Who is in this movie? How do they treat you? How do they influence how you think and feel? What positive or negative life experiences have you had? What have you learned? What haven't you learned? What shouldn't you have learned? What must you unlearn? We know this kind of inventory can feel pretty overwhelming, but it is truly very important to be aware of and understand all its implications because this inventory explains who you are, and why you are as you are. Think of the same questions and consider the same historical development of your partner. What would his or her novel or movie look like? Set time aside to think back, understand, and decide what you might need to build upon or to change.

Consider your life events and skills for life:

- Education
- Life experiences
- Values and morals
- Priorities
- Sexuality
- Alcohol and drugs
- Medicines and illnesses
- Hygiene
- Self-discipline
- Order and organization
- Roles of life
- Religion
- Prayer
- Food / Eating habits
- Social activities
- Athletics
- Importance of TV
- Computers
- Dedication to work
- Showing affection
- Showing and expressing emotions appropriately
- Communication skills
- Problem solving skills
- Friendships
- Honesty
- Money management
- Parents
- Siblings

- Relatives
- Ability to express sorrow
- Ability to forgive

What other experiences of life and skills for living would you add to this list? You may be asking yourself if such an extensive list is necessary and important. How important are these skills as far as readiness for marriage, being "old enough to be married?" If people evaluated their readiness for marriage critically and thoroughly using a list like this, would we have healthier marriages and fewer divorces? If married couples were committed to working on these skills as a couple and have similar and healthy balance, would we have healthier marriages and fewer divorces? Would fewer children have to go through what Sammy and his sisters were going through? I know so! What do you think?

3) What Am I Capable Of?

What personal skills and abilities are truly necessary in a healthy, effective marriage? Ask yourself, "Am I someone who":

- Is a problem solver?
- Is quick to argue?
- Doesn't "get over" the past?
- Is overly sensitive? Isn't sensitive enough?
- Over reacts?
- Shuts down when upset?
- Gets defensive quite quickly?
- Needs to win?
- Is capable of compromise?
- Says "I'm sorry"?
- Is able to forgive?
- Can stay on one topic at a time?
- Gets depressed?
- Has mood swings?
- Drinks too much?

Think of the many skills and qualities you would want in someone you were married to. Think of what traits and habits you would and would not want. Don't worry about how long the list may be. Be extremely thorough and think in terms of the perfect partner. Once you've constructed this extensive list, look at it carefully and decide how many of these you have. Do you come close to being the ideal? If you read your answers, would you call yourself for a date?

4) Absence of Clinical Concerns

When a couple first comes in for couple therapy, they need to understand the difference between couple therapy and individual therapy. A great metaphor to understand this is the example of a doubles tennis team. If the two of them have been arguing a lot, not working out what they need to in order to win, are not enjoying playing together, or are thinking of wanting a different partner; they may decide to dissolve their team. However, on the way there, they pass a sign saying "Coach Meske, Tennis Pro." They decide to give the team one more effort and they go in to meet the coach. The coach says, "Sure, I'll work with you. Let's go outside; I want to see how each of you volley and hit the ball." As I watch, I notice that one or both of them are limping. I tell them to stop and take some x-rays and I discover that one or both of them have a broken leg. Any person with a broken leg is certainly not only unable to play doubles; the reality is that they can't play singles either. The person would first need to heal their own broken leg to play tennis effectively. This healing must occur not only for their own personal game skills, but it would be necessary to be able to bring a healthy partner to the team so that they can truly succeed at developing the game skills necessary to be a healthy, effective, satisfied, winning doubles team. Do you see the connection in a marriage partnership? What are the "broken leg" issues that each person needs to be aware of if these issues exist in their marriage team?

"Broken Leg" Issues that Cripple the Individual and Handicap the Twosome:

- Depression
- Anxiety and panic disorders

- Obsessive compulsive disorders
- Bi-polar disorders
- Explosive disorders
- Addictions and abuses
- Self-centered behaviors
- Disabling phobias
- Mood disorders
- ADD/ADHD issues
- Psychosis
- Brain damage
- Personality disorders

These clinical concerns must be absent or under control for the person and the relationship to succeed. Any such painful, disruptive illnesses need to be recognized, admitted to, and addressed. They require healing because, with such brokenness, the relationship cannot be healthy, satisfying, or effective.

I personally believe that many of these problems are treatable to the point of someone being able to succeed in marriage. The treatment does require a tremendous commitment to therapy! However, getting well and becoming a healthy person can happen with the right efforts.

Now I want to discuss four types of relationship situations a couple needs to be aware of.

1). Compatible (very similar)
2). Compromise (I'm okay doing it your way.)
3). Different but OK. We just can't live together.
4). Different but not OK. Someone is broken and must heal or we can't live together.

1.) Compatible

Compatible means we blend together very easily and wonderfully. You have heard the phrase "opposites attract." The fact is, similarity is what works. As people who are compatible look at the many areas of life they must get along in, they recognize that they will have no problems because of their similarity. When a couple decides to get married, they should figure out which areas of life they experience such compatibility and where they don't. Being compatible will be the ideal. However, if not completely compatible, the couple then needs to live the next situation. (All is not lost!)

2.) Compromise

This is a very necessary skill in all relationships. It is the one that challenges the personal motivation and maturity of each partner. Compromise means being able to respect how each other thinks, feels, and prefers to do something. When couples have different opinions, one of the partners must be able to say, "OK, let's do it your way." Be careful - this is different from saying, "Fine! Do it your way!" and then, walking away upset. Compromise means that someone understands the two possible ways to handle something and is truly willing to do whatever it is that the other person wants to do. This compromise should be something both are able to do at different times in their relationship so there is a fair balance.

3.) We're Different, but OK. We just can't live together.

Here is the bird and fish analogy. Both creatures are perfectly fine and okay in their own unique ways and preferences; they can even be great friends; they just can't live together. There are many areas of life when this "different but okay" can be true. Far too often, couples want to argue about these differences. They choose to live together in pain and conflict rather than compromise or admit that living together isn't a good idea. Because of their vow, they should be making every possible effort to effectively compromise! This would mean making a big change in someone's life, requiring some tremendous effort. The person would have to make sure that he or she can do this without anger, resentment, depression, or frustration.

4.) Different, but not OK. We can't possibly live together unless major change not compromise occurs.

This brings us back to the clinical concerns, the "broken legs" that cannot be lived with, and shouldn't be attempted to be lived with for very long. Anytime these differences, these unhealthy patterns, are present, the vow means you should offer to stay around and work with this partner and their problems. However, this effort should only last so long; and only if the unhealthy partner truly commits themself to the healing, changing, and growing that are necessary. Failure to be strong and convicted in this not only results in a great deal of mental and emotional pain in the partners and their relationship, but the toll is also very great on the children.

It is very understandable, as well as very painfully difficult, to know when and for how long something is tolerable and can be effectively coped with. We must know when living with someone is intolerable and the consequences are too severe. Most of us would need help at such times, figuring out if we've done all we could and when it's time to say, "I won't live like this any longer." This is usually very difficult but often times very necessary!

I always emphasize with a couple who reach this point that, even if they can't succeed as a couple, certainly they should work hard and succeed as parents. Effectively co-parenting for the rest of their lives, even co-grandparenting, needs to be seen as crucial for the sake of their children. The two people must be held accountable for all that is at stake and how much everyone stands to lose. The couple should work very hard at how to work together effectively as parents! They should seek a therapist or a pastoral counselor to help them and help the children.

Understanding this, we're ready to get into the many other ingredients for a healthy, effective, satisfying relationship. You have now sensed how tremendously important the *first ingredient is – two healthy, ready, "old enough to be married" individuals.* What are the many other ingredients, skills, areas of life, couples must have, do, and share so that their marriage is healthy, satisfying, and effective?

Commitment

This is certainly one of the most crucial ingredients. We're in a society that encourages the thinking, "If it feels good, do it; if it doesn't feel good, get away from it." In so many areas of life, this is not a healthy message. One of these areas is marriage. When it doesn't feel good, a healthy couple values their commitment and focuses on changing and coping. Commitment means that, because of the vow you took on your wedding day, you and your spouse are going to work through and deal effectively with what is wrong, what is missing, or what doesn't seem to be working. "In good times and in bad," a vow was made. It's time to live the Serenity Prayer.

Grant me the courage to change what can be changed,
To cope with what can't be changed, and
The ability to know the difference.

Sadly, this is not the attitude and mind set some people have about marriage. Far too often, people leave their marriage too early or live unhappily, angrily, unhealthily, and frustrated too long, or they eventually get involved with someone else or something else that replaces their partner. When this happens, the pain and damage to the marriage are horrible. The pain and damage to the children are horrible. One or both of the partners are failing to live up to their vow. They are failing to live up to the commitment that means "I am here to work with you, to grow with you, to change what I need to change, to learn what I need to learn, and to cope effectively with you in those areas of life we can't change." Is divorce ever the healthy decision? Yes, certainly, but not too quickly! Not until serious efforts have been made to heal and to try to grow back together.

Many times, people wait too long to seek help. One partner may have been suggesting they seek help, but the resistance of the other results in therapy not happening when it should. Far too often I see this resistance continue for a very long time, and then, when the other partner reaches the "I won't live like this any longer" point, then the resistant partner gets the wake-up call. What a tragic process, because now the fed-up partner may have lost their motivation to keep trying and their commitment energy feels spent.

In such situations, I encourage the couple to try anyway. I suggest that the one who feels like it's too late be the one to make some efforts for a reasonable period of time and see if the feelings return. Avoid making crucial, life-changing decisions based on how you feel at this time. See if, in time and with some changes, your feelings change. This is a very difficult time for both of you – one has finally gotten concerned, and the other is resentful and frustrated that it took so long. You can certainly see how much will be necessary if some healing and growing are to occur. Believe me, it can happen. However, this long painful pattern has done damage to the commitment and motivation. I work very hard with people to try to rebuild this commitment and motivation. It can be done.

Realistic and Appropriate Expectations

Before we get involved in a committed relationship, it is really important and valuable if we have a clear understanding of what is expected of us in the relationship and what we can expect of the other person. It seems that far too often people get into a relationship, take on certain roles, and are surprised to discover pretty quickly that what is expected of them and what they expect of the other are not what they anticipated. As you can imagine, these kinds of discoveries lead to tremendous pain, conflict, and damage. In hindsight, people get this wake-up call and realize they should have understood these expectations *before* getting married. They should have evaluated how appropriate and realistic their expectations were. They should have discussed whether or not each of them were motivated to live up to these expectations and needs before getting married. This is certainly the desired way to approach marriage and determine if the marriage is a good idea or not.

However, it does seem realistic to say that, no matter how much effort may have been made before marriage, the majority of us discover many marital expectations, needs, and requirements *after* marriage. The realities of all it takes to make a healthy, satisfying, and effective marriage become much more apparent after the wedding, as we are living within the relationship. This is when we learn about and discover all sorts of expectations. This discovery may also lead to recognizing the need for professional help. So very often, I see people in therapy who wouldn't be there, who sometimes wouldn't need to be there, if they hadn't "complicated" their life by getting married or having children. As soon as they got themselves involved in one or both of these roles, they discovered what they weren't ready to do. So now what? Are they going to be mature enough to commit themselves to the task of learning how to live up to the necessary expectations of the roles they entered into? I believe we have an obligation, because of the marital vow, to make the efforts the marriage and family life call for. People are counting on us and have the right to count on us!

What expectations are you bringing to your relationship? Are the expectations realistic and appropriate? Do each of you know how to live up to them? Is each of you willing to learn how to live up to them? This is such a terribly important piece for a healthy, effective, satisfying marriage. The question is, "now that we know each other's needs and expectations, are we committed to working on them?"

Communication Skills and Problem-Solving Skills

This is another major, crucial ingredient for marriage. Do you and your spouse have good communications skills? Do you and your spouse know how to problem-solve effectively? What are good, effective communication and problem-solving skills? Let's make a list!

1. Don't interrupt and don't ramble. Self-discipline is needed to listen, to work at hearing and not responding until the other is finished. Conversely, making the same point in multiple ways or going on and on make it very difficult to let you finish.
2. Learn to ask questions rather than making statements. If you take a minute to convert what you want to say into a question, you will really promote dialogue. Then, be quiet. Wait. Don't start explaining why you asked the question.
3. Avoid responding defensively. This is probably one of the toughest to learn. We desperately want to defend or explain our behavior. Instead, think about the much greater value in responding apologetically or understandingly to the other's emotions rather than defensively. For example, "Well, I'll try very hard not to have you feel that way again," or, "I really do care that you took it that way," or, "I'll try to do better." You don't have to agree with what was said to respond in these ways; you're just demonstrating you care how the other person is feeling and agreeing to make an effort to make the changes they are seeking.
4. Voice tone!! Voice tone, facial expression, and body language alter every message. How often do these non-verbals affect your relationship? Voice tone is crucial. Tone influences how you are coming across. It conveys soft and

gentle versus hard and harsh. It conveys sarcasm or respect. It influences both your message and how you are seen by the other. This is a huge element in effective communication. It often requires that you make yourself *sound* different than you feel. Don't wreck the message by your delivery.

5. Be more concerned about how your partner feels and how the relationship is than winning. It ought to be more important what you two do from now on than who was right yesterday. Learning from an experience is more important than being right! Also, what about those times when you're both right, just different? Remember the part about compromise?
6. Have the ability to get to "Well, what should we do from now on?" as quickly as possible. In couple relationships, getting stuck in the negative too long is a major problem. To connect as a team as soon as possible and to address what you can do to win together are crucial abilities two people must have for a relationship to be healthy. How often and for how long do the two of you keep going over the past? When does this become a waste of time? What is either of you waiting for? Are you needing to win and get your way, or are you wanting to get back together? Are you going to be teammates or opponents? "Okay, so from now on, let's agree that…" This works best!
7. Stay on one point. Going from topic to topic, old ones as well as recent ones, results in nothing getting accomplished. This topic to topic mistake is called snowballing. Instead, define the topic, allow time for each person to address it, and say "Well, what can we do from now on?" Don't move on to another topic until you've resolved and closed this one.
8. Learn how to react appropriately when your partner has reacted inappropriately. It's so easy to react to anger, sarcasm, and silence with anger, sarcasm, and silence. This is what we call a fight. Someone must remain composed, and if you sustain this long enough, the other

person may kick-in. If not, at least you haven't fueled the problem and made it worse. It is not uncommon that one of the partners must defuse the moment so things don't escalate. When a couple is getting along and enjoying one another, this is a good time to agree on the principles and behavior that will work and be effective when they are not getting along and not enjoying one another. Establishing some solid, effective ways to act and not to act when all is well means you will be prepared to know what to do and not to do when all is not well. You should be able to call upon these effective ways and hold one another accountable for them at those challenging times. "Time out. Let's take a break, let me calm down, I need a work-out, let's take time to write about what's going on…" These are great de-escalating techniques to try before you get back to the issue.

9. Recognize when the daily schedule you're living is inherently unhealthy to your relationship and, by its very nature, doesn't allow time for the communication that needs to happen. And then, do something about it. Far too often, I hear people complain how horrible their schedules are. Well then, why not sit down, look at it, and change it? Make time to take care of one another's emotional, physical, and companionship needs. If your schedule doesn't have blocks of time when you can talk with one another, then you'll need to schedule it! Put the time to talk right on your calendar – schedule it.
10. Commit to *Revisiting*. There are certainly times when a time-out is warranted or there just wasn't enough time to finish and resolve an issue. Perhaps your emotions or mood were interfering with effective communication. The point is that you didn't resolve something or reach a sense of closure, and you didn't reach some agreement that guarantees it won't happen again. Consequently, you are not finished! When this happens, and it often does, what is called for is the commitment and the ability to *revisit*. This means we must return to the topic and promise each other

to respect the importance of resolving the issue as soon as possible. Both people should look at their calendars and schedule a time to revisit the issue.

11. Other communication techniques are letter writing, sharing a journal at home that you both use to share notes and thoughts with one another, using the phone if having space helps you, texting, email, carrier pigeon (just seeing if you're paying attention). Become committed to the techniques that work for you.

As you can see, there are numerous communication skills for effective problem-solving that couples must be willing to learn and to use. They are not easy. They are not natural skills someone automatically brings into marriage; they must be learned and practiced. Also, we must unlearn ineffective, inappropriate habits that just don't work. With the right motivation and efforts, effective communication and problem-solving skills can be learned and can become an effective part of your life. Expect them of yourself and expect them of your partner. These skills are crucial and well worth the effort.

The ability to be sorrowful, to ask for forgiveness, and to be able to forgive

Years ago, in the movie *Love Story*, there was a line: "Love means never having to say you're sorry." Well, that must be one of the most ridiculous statements ever made! Love means being able to say that you are sorry and being able to ask for forgiveness. Although we should try not to fail, not to hurt, and not to disappoint our partner, the reality is that there will be those times that we do fail, do hurt, and do disappoint. The nature of our humanness is that we are imperfect and will stumble. At such times, healthy partners are able to say, "I am sorry; please forgive me." Let's look at what these powerful words mean. What should being sorry really mean? What would being able to forgive mean?

As with many words and statements in our culture, they have been misused, exaggerated, said prematurely, and have lost their intended meaning. For example, "I'm sorry" can be said very quickly, with very little thinking, just because someone wants you to say it. Consequently, how meaningful is it? "I'm sorry" should mean "I feel bad about what I did; it matters to me that I upset you," and "I don't intend to do that again." These are the thoughts and intentions that should accompany "I'm sorry." "Please forgive me" should mean "please give me another chance and let me regain your trust in me." The partner who has done the hurting, upsetting, or disappointing needs to be able to express this sorrow and ask for forgiveness. These first two steps set the stage for the third step – the ability to forgive.

What is forgiveness? What does it mean to be able to forgive? First of all, let's remove the notion that being able to forget is part of being able to forgive. Being able to forget would truly be a wonderful blessing, but since it is unlikely, let's make sure that we don't make it a criteria for forgiving. So then, what is it?

Forgiveness is the ability to look at oneself, or at another, and understand that because something painful happened, that some mistake was made, that person is still a good person, worthwhile, and deserving of pardon. It means being able to quit bringing up the mistake again and again. It means being able to regard the pains of the past as experiences we learn and grow from. It means being able to accept and believe in the person's sorrow and good intentions. Forgiveness means being able to not be stuck in the pains, angers, guilts, and regrets of the past; but to live in the present with energy and to approach the future with optimism.

Couples need to be able to do these steps when the disappointing, betraying, hurtful, or aggravating times occur. Surely every couple makes efforts to prevent these negative times but, come on; we all know there is no such thing as perfection when it comes to two people living life together. Therefore, "I'm sorry, please forgive me, and I forgive you" must be part of every healthy, satisfying, effective marriage.

There is another piece of forgiveness that needs to be addressed at this time. It is the potential fourth step in the forgiving process – reconciliation: "I still want to be with you." For example, some painful event happens. The process would be:

1. "I am truly sorry."

2. “Please forgive me.”
3. “I forgive you.” And now,
4. “I want us to continue our life together.” This is reconciliation.

There may come the time, for whatever reasons, where the fourth step doesn’t occur. Instead of reconciliation, one partner says, “We must move on with our own personal lives and no longer share the journey as a couple.” This is a very painful, overwhelmingly difficult moment for a couple, a moment couple’s therapy tries to prevent. Unfortunately, there are times this needs to occur and the people need to move on and learn to live effectively as single people, while remaining effective as co-parents. It’s important to respect this conclusion for some couples. If the right efforts have been made and this ending must occur, then acknowledge the effort but also find peace in moving on. If there are children, put a great deal of energy into being effective, cooperative parents. Don’t let the divorce process and whatever may have damaged the marriage contaminate the rest of your lives as parents. I understand how difficult and challenging this is. I have worked with many couples trying to achieve this cooperating goal. It is very difficult. The couple must regard the children and the co-parenting moments as more important than their personal feelings. This takes a great deal of work, but extremely worthwhile work. Be committed to it.

Fidelity

Earlier we discussed the ingredient “commitment,” the promise to work with one another when things aren’t going well. Fidelity is different. Fidelity specifically means “I will not betray you sexually and emotionally. I will reserve the sexual and emotional intimacies of marriage for you and me.” Infidelity includes inappropriate behavior between a spouse and another person, self indulgent pornography, or an inappropriate emotional connection, and sharing with another person outside of the marriage when such connections and sharing belong within the marriage. Fidelity means that a spouse is determined not to betray their partner. It means not permitting anything to go on in one’s personal life that would hurt their partner.

Fidelity means living up to the appropriate expectations of one's spouse and the expectation of a healthy marriage.

In a society that promotes "if your needs are going unmet, get them met where you can," we must be careful what we allow to influence the choices we make. In a society where morality is often contrary to our values and morals, we could easily lose sight of what is right or wrong. If spouses aren't committed to working on whatever may be wrong or missing in their relationship they may choose some behavior that may be satisfying and temporarily makes up for what is wrong or missing, but in doing so commit infidelity.

A couple should realize that there are many ways to prevent an infidelity from happening. Certainly, the most obvious would be that the two people are doing a good job at taking care of one another's needs. They are content and satisfied with their relationship.

However, when this isn't true, when contentment and satisfaction are missing, it doesn't justify taking one's needs elsewhere. What is or isn't going on in the marital relationship may explain why someone may be vulnerable to going elsewhere with their needs. However, this does not justify the wrong choice! There is no legitimate excuse for infidelity. Explanation? Maybe. Excuse? Never! Fidelity still comes down to the decision-making of an individual. The person is to be held accountable for having made the wrong decision. Blaming someone else for their decision is unfair and incorrect.

Also, the infidelity choice may have nothing to do with the partner. Many times, the partner may be a wonderful, need-meeting partner who is truly trying to do his or her best. The struggling spouse may even truly love and value their partner. Their decision to be unfaithful happens, not because of the spouse, but because of the unfaithful person's own self-centeredness, their own selfishness, their own impulsivity, their own lack of good judgment, or their personal struggles interfering with their life.

Notice the two possible situations a couple must look at. Has the unsatisfying marital relationship created a vulnerability that needs to be addressed as a couple, or is the reason the person's own unhealthiness and brokenness that he or she needs to address personally? Both require a great deal of work and forgiveness as a couple, but the second situation places additional work and responsibility on the individual. Make sure you understand these two situations and the difference between them.

When infidelity happens in a marriage, the couple who wants to work to survive this event very often can do so. There is a great deal of personal and couple therapy this couple can do together to discover if they can rebuild their relationship. Can they convey enough sorrow and sensitivity? Can forgiveness and reconciliation occur? Can trust be rebuilt? Can history be depowered and not be allowed to overwhelm them? Can they face together and accomplish together all that they need to in order to happily, effectively, and lovingly continue life's journey together? Can they possibly get closer to one another than they have ever been before? Yes, I have seen all of these happen!

If you are struggling with moving-on after some damaging, painful event, maybe this process will assist you. However, think about the value of having some therapist or pastoral counselor help you through the process.

Healing From a Painful Event

When an affair or any damaging event has occurred, a process for healing and growing must be found. I think these elements are crucial for the healing:

- A tremendous sense of sorrow from the failing spouse. There must be frequent expression of this sorrow; the failing spouse must be able to convey their pain and their deep regret for causing the other such pain. The message of deep sorrow and determination to never cause this pain again must be given often and gently.
- A level of understanding in the failing spouse of how painful this event has been to the spirit of the partner. This understanding must be verbalized and demonstrated by gentle patience and by expressing their emotional and physical awareness of what the hurt partner must be going through. "I cry when I think about how often you must cry" or "I get sick to my stomach when I think about how angry you must be with me" or "I can't sleep when I realize you can't sleep." Being able to empathize is crucial!
- Write a letter of sorrow and reassurance to the partner who has been hurt. Then, when the person they need to reassure them is not around, having something to read can be phenomenally beneficial. The person can read and reread it to help cope through the day and see if he or she still needs to talk when the spouse gets home. If the person who did the hurting can add this to the first two suggestions, the healing and growing process seems to move along better.
- An attitude in the hurt partner that enables him or her to forgive and to be able to move on after what has occurred. This is the combined ability to forgive and reconcile. It is truly a two-part process and two very different challenges. Believe that one or both are capable of being done.
- The two people must have the ability to decide how much detail is valuable. This must be carefully thought out and evaluated on both a personal and interpersonal basis. Each party should process these issues with a therapist before making a decision.

- Individually and as a couple, they must develop the problem-solving skills that will enable them to effectively get through tough times. They need to identify what changes need to be made and what is fair to expect. As they are trying to move on with their lives, there may be major changes needing to be made – give up a hobby, end a friendship, leave a job, move from a neighborhood, find a new fitness club, etc. There will be occasions that will trigger thoughts, memories, and emotions that the two people will need to decide the best way to handle and help each other at such times. What needs to be said? What shouldn't be said? What should I do or should we agree not to do? When a tough memory is raised, how effective are our personal and couple problem-solving skills?
- Their relationship must have enough good times, satisfying times, and elements in it that strengthen it and give them something to truly value, appreciate, and look forward to. The couple's spiritual and philosophical attitudes about life and the journey play very important roles here. Our lives now and in the future, as grandparents for example, should also be taken into consideration. My experience has been that people who share spirituality - the value of prayer, the messages of Jesus, some Higher Power connection – tend to heal more quickly through the tough times.
- As a couple, they must have the ability to go back to before the mistake and learn what went wrong. They must be able to look at themselves, at each other, and be honest about what was going on or not going on in their marriage and turn this understanding into the opportunity to grow personally and together.

Shared Fun and Mutual Interests

When you think about what contributes toward two people becoming friends, what do you come up with? And, if the friendship lasts and even grows, what factors seem to explain this bond between two people? We could probably come up with a number of answers, but two of them would be the ability to have fun together and to have shared fun to look forward to. The two people share mutual interests and goals - things they enjoy talking about and experiencing together in the present, as well as in the future.

As an individual, how do you have fun? What activities do you look forward to? How often do you experience them? When was the last time you did them? Remember the list you made when working on the six emotional needs? Look at it again and ask yourself how many of these you share with your spouse. How are the two of you doing as far as sharing fun times, having enjoyable interests, and having things to look forward to together?

Recall how important these ingredients were when you were dating. If you hadn't enjoyed each other's company and didn't have things to share and look forward to, you wouldn't have continued to date. What were those fun activities and interests? Do they continue in your relationship? Do they need to be rejuvenated? Do you need to create new ones? Yes, create new ones! This can be done.

If shared fun and mutual interests are missing, create them. Consciously identify new things to try, to learn together, to experience to see if you could enjoy them. It's okay to have to make the effort. If you wait for something to be naturally spontaneous it might not happen! As long as you can both agree that these ingredients for a good relationship are important, what difference does it make if you have to work a little harder to find them and to experience them? Think about the alternative... how attractive does that sound to you?

Fun and mutual interests not only bring energy and enjoyment to the relationship and marriage, they also give you reasons to make-up. When you have things to look forward to and enjoy, you want to put conflicts or differences or upset feelings out of the way as soon as possible. Fun and mutual interests become motivators. So, once again, what do you and your spouse think about all of this? And, what are the two of you going to do about it?

Humor

Life is certainly an interesting, diverse, rewarding, and difficult journey. There are the ups and downs of daily living that make up our lives. When the moments are fun and interesting, these are the easy times to relax, laugh, and have fun. These are the times when kidding around comes naturally; when finding humor in life and joking with each other take very little effort.

Now, without sounding unrealistic, is it possible to also be able to laugh at oneself? Can you find humor in some of the "mishap" times in life? Can you make it safe to even laugh at each other? Come on, we all know we have those times when you ask yourself "What was that all about?" or, "Did I really just say that?" And so, sometimes, you must be able to sit back and realize, "Goodness, aren't we something?"

Schedule and Priorities

One of the major problems I see in individual, couple, or family therapy is the schedule people have designed for themselves. Whatever understanding and potential growth are identified in a session, the fact that people walk out of the office and go right back into the schedule they have been living before they started therapy proves to be a major setback. The amount of time a couple has for one another is similar to watering the flower garden. If there is no time to nourish the flowers with water, they die. So too in marriage, the absence of adequate time to enjoy one another and to work at issues affecting the relationship result in the relationship "dying". The problem with this obvious statement isn't that people don't understand and recognize it; the problem is the failure to truly do something about it and remain committed to the change. The real issue is will you truly do something about your schedule and priorities?

This schedule, the demands of life you put on yourself, are crucial in all areas of wellness—personal, marital, and family. The discipline needed to keep your schedule from running your life, from getting in the way of time needed to be close and happy with one another, becomes a major concern for any healthy relationship. Along with this discipline comes one's priorities -what really matters?

Theoretically, most people probably know what the answers should be when asked "What really matters to you? What are the true priorities of life?" However, knowing them, admitting to them, and actually living them are truly very different. So, what are you willing to do about this reality?

There are probably many valuable and important activities, responsibilities, and expectations on your current calendar. To adjust your schedule so that your relationship has the time it needs will mean giving up some valuable or fun things. It may mean restructuring your work schedule. It may mean talking together every Sunday night agreeing how the week will go and not go. It may mean saying no to some wonderful activity your child wants to participate in. It may mean cutting back on some meaningful volunteer work or church project. What may need to happen so that you have more time for one another? What are you willing to remove from your schedule? What are you willing to limit in your child's activities? What are you willing to put on your calendar, to actually schedule as "our time?"

As with so many of the ingredients for a successful relationship, actually following through is not easy, but it's essential! Are you motivated and disciplined enough to do so? If so, talk about a time when you will sit down and re-evaluate and change your schedule. Literally, write on your calendar when the two of you will revamp your schedule and how you will stay committed to it. Discuss specific priorities you will stay committed to. These are truly some very crucial "homework assignments." Follow through.

Affection and Nurturing

Isn't it fun and very little effort to hold and cuddle with a baby or a little child? Whether the child is happy or sad, smiling or crying, isn't it pretty spontaneous how we pick up this child and relish the joy or make efforts to soothe the pain?

In Transactional Analysis we talk about the Parent, Adult, and Child parts of us. The Child is the part that experiences feelings and emotions. This is not referring to immaturity. As with the parent part, the part that nurtures and serves as a conscience, and the Adult part, the part that thinks and reasons, the Child part is within us throughout our life. It's the part that laughs or cries, feels happy or sad, loved or unloved, appreciated or not appreciated, safe or unsafe - all the feelings and emotions of life lie within our child part.

In your relationship with one another, how effectively are you taking care of the Child in each other? How do you do it? Do you touch, hug, kiss? Do you verbally nurture each other? Do you write notes, send cards? Do you do special things for each other? Do you give gifts? How do you express affection and show nurturing to your spouse? How does he or she do these for you? Would each of you like to suggest some ways to one another that would improve the nurturing? Gary Chapman's *The Five Love Languages* is excellent reading material for a couple.

A couple may discover and need to admit that one or both of them failed to learn how to nurture, how to take care of the child inside of them or the child inside someone else. One's history is very significant in this issue. If someone failed to experience their own child part being cared for and nurtured, they probably won't know how to ask for such caring, nor how to give it. Even if they know what could be done to care for the child inside themselves or someone else, they won't be comfortable doing so. What can be done about this?

There are multiple treatment goals and objectives when a couple enters couple therapy. A major goal is that they learn to do a much better job taking care of the child in each other. Touching, holding hands, hugging, giving compliments, doing a favor, sharing words of appreciation, a flower, a gentle kiss, a phone call... what would the two of you add to the list? There are so many different ways to care for our child, ways each couple needs to talk about and to discover what works best for them.

I want you to be optimistic and positive about "caring for the child" in one another. You can definitely learn how to do this much better, more satisfyingly. It might feel clumsy and uncomfortable at first, but as long as it's sincere and has some consistency, this is a wonderful, loving thing to do. The receiving spouse should be grateful and appreciative. The spouse making the effort should be proud and recognize the value of what he or she is learning to do. No matter what your history or level of comfort or discomfort, learning to care for the child in someone else and to let someone care for the child in you will become more and more comfortable and rewarding in your relationships with time and effort.

Intimacy and Sexuality

It is very important to distinguish between nurturing, affection, intimacy, and sexuality. They are very different and they are to be lived very differently. Too often people believe that hugs, touches, kisses, and statements of caring and appreciation must always lead to being sexual and physically intimate. It's as though affection is regarded as foreplay and that things are supposed to progress to sexual pleasure and sexual intimacies. Affections and nurturing moments can be pleasurable and feel intimate.

If you are a couple where sex and physical intimacies have been missing for quite a while or aren't frequent enough or mutually satisfying enough, there are multiple things you can do about this.

- Know your body, know what excites and pleasures you
- Know your partner's body and what pleasures him or her
- Be able to talk about these and even to instruct one another
- Find out if making sex and intimacy satisfying for both of you is an important goal for your relationship. Ask each other if taking time to grow in this area is truly worthwhile
- Work at lessening inhibitions, discomforts, and any historical negatives that get in the way of enjoying sex
- Agree on what the two of you value and enjoy. Don't be overly influenced by some societal message or from how you hear others talk
- Be careful of being unrealistically influenced by mass media and societal messages. So often, these are misleading, unrealistic, and very damaging to on-going relationships. It's important to be cautious about what you are comparing your relationship to
- Be willing to be creative, to explore new intimacies with your spouse

Emotional Intimacy is the sharing of oneself with another in non-physical, non-sexual ways. Emotional intimacy is present between two people when:

- They tell one another what they are thinking and feeling
- They look at one another when talking
- They sense they know one another

- They make it clear that it matters to each of them how they make one another feel
- They share fun, joyful times
- They share painful, unhappy times
- They support each other during struggling times
- They look forward to being with each other
- Sorrow and forgiveness occur when necessary
- They work together to prevent boring, distancing, painful habits and routines
- They problem-solve effectively together
- They… (what would you say?)
- They don't … (what would you say?)

When these things happen, the couple has achieved emotional intimacy.

Sexual intimacy is the sharing of oneself in physical, sexual ways that are different from, and more erotically intense, than physical affection and nurturing, which stimulate more of the emotional intimacy. Behaviors like hand-holding, walking with your arms around one another, hugs, gentle facial, shoulder, or back touches, and words of endearment and appreciation fall into the *categories of emotional intimacy and physical affection and nurturing.* The combination of these two is crucial and phenomenally important for deep, meaningful relationships. As a matter of fact, we might say that emotional intimacy and physical affection and nurturing *must* be present in order for sexual intimacy to happen. Think about the powerful and wonderful combination of emotional intimacy + physical affection and nurturing + sexual intimacy. What a tremendous equation for marital success!

The reason this important element of marriage has not been addressed earlier is that I wanted to emphasize how many other elements of marriage must be satisfying and fulfilling for sexual intimacy to feel right. Sexual intimacy and satisfaction is very often the combination of multiple other elements of the relationship that need to be in a good place. Certainly there are times when just wanting sexual pleasure is the motivator. Well, enjoy! As a couple, set time to talk about what you need that leads you to a more satisfying, loving, intimate sexual life.

Before ending this section of the book, I'd like you to read the letter I give to couples when they first start couple therapy. I believe it captures the attitude couples should have about why they need to work together on their marriage and what they must accomplish from their efforts. Keep in mind that a couple can use the messages of this letter even if they're not in therapy. Just figure out what you as a couple need to do.

Letter for Couples Who Wish to Benefit from Therapy

You have come in to meet with me today and have told me your story of what's wrong with your marriage and why you are unhappy. You have either stated quite clearly and strongly that you want your marriage to improve and you want to work at it, or you have come across quite unsure and undecided as to how important this relationship is to you. However, since you are here, I am going to take the position that therapy will begin and you will benefit from therapy, one way or the other. If you are going to choose to work with me, you need to understand how I approach couple therapy – what I believe must happen and what you need to be willing to do.

At some point in your life as a couple, you decided that making a commitment to each other was a good idea. Some reasons, whether solid ones or not, led you to decide to spend your life together. You said something about "in good times and in bad, in sickness and in health, until death do us part."

Well, here you are, and it's feeling to you like something has been seriously wrong in your marriage. Unfortunately, we sometimes wait far too long before we acknowledge how bad things are getting. However, here you are! Let's see what healing needs to occur and what learning, growing and changing need to occur. Let's work together and see what we can accomplish.

This healing and growing will probably take on various forms. You need to understand these concepts:

- Healing and Learning
- Healing and Changing
- Healing and Growing

Healing means recognizing what is unhealthy in yourself, in your partner, and in your relationship and making it well. It also means being able to be sorry and empathetic and able to forgive so you can start again and move on. Learning, changing, and growing mean becoming educated and knowledgeable to the skills of marriage and making them yours. Which must you do?

If you sense depression, low self-esteem, selfishness, anger, addictions, unreasonable expectations, lying, unforgiveness, or other issues, you need healing. Without being personally well, well enough to be a healthy partner, how could you be capable of a healthy marriage?

Marriage requires numerous skills, capabilities, and strengths. I believe couples must know how to communicate, problem-solve, nurture, be affectionate, have fun, control voice tone, not overreact, and other skills. You may need to learn many of these. You may need to un-learn bad habits. These things can be learned and must happen in your relationship.

Are you willing to change? Are you willing to stop some things and start others? Are you willing to work very hard? I am inviting you to

- Honestly look at yourself
- Honestly look at your relationship
- Figure out what must change
- Work hard to make these happen

If you do these, you will either discover how to make and have a wonderful relationship together or you will come to realize that you must move on from one another. But, if you have children, you must be able to work together effectively for your children and remain effective co-parents.

Read this letter over a couple of times. It is so important that you understand what I believe the focus of therapy is, how people need to behave and work while in therapy, and that therapy is a process of changing – either actually changing some behaviors and results, or changing our ability to cope more effectively. In both cases, when a couple works this hard to make changes, they are then capable of discovering a more effective and healthy life together. I look forward to working with you on this journey of wellness.

So, this ends the section on the building an emotionally healthy marriage. Hopefully you can see the value in considering all of this information, both as a couple in marriage or as a couple considering marriage. Certainly this is a great deal of work and requires a consistent effort. What in life that is worthwhile and important doesn't require work and effort? God bless you as you focus and work together. The effort is truly worthwhile!

Following are several exercises to use as a couple to help you focus on changing and growing together.

Couple's Exercise: Six Emotional Needs

When reading the material on our emotional needs, it seems crucial to do a good job at taking care of these on both a personal and interpersonal basis. Let's review how:

- I see myself taking care of them
- I see my partner taking care of them
- I see us taking care of them together

1. Sense of Security

2. Sense of Accomplishment and Purpose

3. Positive Self Image

4. Satisfying, Healthy Relationships

5. Taking Care of Personal and Interpersonal Unfinished Business

6. The Ability to Have Fun and Anticipate Fun

Couple's Exercise: Affection and Sexual Intimacy

When I think about the kinds of affection you want from me

The kinds of affection I want you to know I would like from you

Let's be open and honest here, either verbally or in writing, about a number of things. Talk in terms of "more of, lots of, less of, how to, what feels good." Be specific.

1. Our kissing:

2. Touches: (where I like to be touched, how to touch me, where I like touching you…)

3. Some physical things I want you to be aware of: (hygiene, shaving, clothes you wear, how you go to bed, weight, roughness, too passive…)

4. Our sexual frequency: (what I would like, what you would like, can we come to a comfortable agreement?)

5. For me to be more receptive to our sexual relationship, what I want you to be sensitive to and to respect is…

6. Am I struggling with any insecurities, self-doubt, concerns, and thoughts about you that interfere with my ability to be relaxed in our sexual relationship?

7. Are there any sexual activities you or I wish we did more often?

8. Are there any sexual activities you and I are okay with but we need to talk more about?

9. There are some sexual activities I just am not comfortable with, and I would like us to agree on not expecting them in our relationship.

Any other thoughts, comments, wishes, or concerns?

Couple's Exercise: Couple Time and Personal Time

We understand the importance of:

- the schedule we have in our life. Are we really managing it or is it managing us?
- rearranging our priorities – what does this mean we must do?
- having time to truly take care of the needs of one another – what should we each commit to?
- recognizing what is really going on in our life and addressing it before it becomes critical – let's get specific.
- following through on what it means to take good care of our relationship, and the needs of our children, and then our own personal time, keeping in mind that a healthy balance does not mean *equal time.* What promises are we going to make to one another?

1. Are both of us satisfied with the amount of time and the quality of time we have with each other?

2. What changes, even commitment, would we like to see the two of us make? Think of some routine ways we can improve the quality time and fun time with each other. What do we share together as ways to have fun?

3. If we realize mutual interests are missing, what are some we can develop?

4. We both know that personal time is an important part of a healthy relationship and of being a healthy person. What do the two of us need to agree on so that personal time is a positive part of our relationship, not a negative?

5. Has the way we spend our personal time and how we have paid attention to our couple time caused any trouble for our relationship? If so, talk about what changes we are committed to making. Don't get stuck on "what it has been like," but spend more time on "from now on…"

Couple's Exercise: Patterns and Behaviors

The point of these questions is to enable each of you to get specific about changes needing to be made.

1. What patterns of mine – my behaviors, thoughts, thinking patterns, and emotions – make it difficult to live with me?

2. How would my spouse answer this about me?

3. How would I answer this about my spouse?

Couple's Exercise: Problem-Solving and Communication

When you and I look at the list of skills and key ingredients for a healthy marriage:

1. Which ones do I think we do well at?

2. Which ones do I think we do poorly at?

3. Can we agree to work at what needs to be done from now on?

Remember, old habits are not broken or changed quickly. You are going to need to help each other. If things like interrupting, yelling, becoming defensive, snowballing, changing the topic, criticizing, or shutting down and refusing to talk are already habits in your relationship, you will need to be personally committed to the effort to change yourself and also be receptive to your partner's efforts at reminding you.

4. Are there certain areas in our life that cause us the most trouble? Let's specifically identify areas such as kids, finances, sex, friends, our schedules, moments when we're tired, issues with certain people, or when we have had too much to drink. These are the boulders! What can we do to remove them?

Let's be committed to always try to use the ideas we have learned here. When working on issues or situations in our life when we need to problem-solve, let's talk with and work with each other *adult to adult* and practice all the effective communication and problem-solving skills that come with being effective together.

Couple's Exercise: Respect and Appreciation

What is respect? How do I show it?

Showing respect and appreciation, being complimentary, and not being critical are usually greatly influenced by living up to one another's expectations.

1. Let me tell you where you are doing a wonderful job at living up to my expectations.

2. At times, there seem to be moments of frustration, anger, disappointment, or let down as to how I am doing or not doing something you're counting on. Pick a few areas in our life where you would want me to function differently than I am.

3. When we are upset with one another, do we speak or act in ways that come across so disrespectfully that we need to make some changes and make some promises to one another?

4. What can we agree upon so that complimenting, appreciating, and showing how we value each other come across to one another more often?

What are the problems? (the boulders)

What do we each need to promise to do?
(to start, to stop, to take care of from our past)

Remember, a boulder can represent something happening, on-going, that keeps us apart, hurts us, or something missing that pushes us apart.

Couple's Exercise: Wellness in Our Marriage

1. After reading this chapter and thinking about couple and marital signs of wellness, how is a good marriage supposed to feel? How is a good marriage supposed to look as far as how the two people behave and treat each other?

2. Must I feel "in love" to say "I love you?" How much emphasis or importance do we place on feelings? What does the mass media and the societal messages say about the importance of feelings? "If it feels good…" Do we agree with this?

3. Do we frequently bring up painful events from the past and get stuck on looking back? Let's make a plan to limit dwelling on the past. Maybe we can set up two chairs in the basement and go sit downstairs whenever we go backwards?

4. How safe do we make it for each other to talk about anything?

5. Can we use these images to help us?

A) Identify the "flowers of life," the parts that are beautiful and bring you joy in your relationship?

What are the painful Issues?

B) The pieces of our life must fit together. How does all that each of us is and all that makes up our lives fit together?

C) How do we blend our roles as parent, adult, and child?

<u>MY:</u> Parent Adult Child	(and all the possible parent, adult, and child transactions)	<u>YOUR:</u> Parent Adult Child

I'm OK, You're OK, by Thomas Harris, chapters 2, 3, 4, and 8, will be very helpful.

D) When and how do we mend a broken heart?

E)

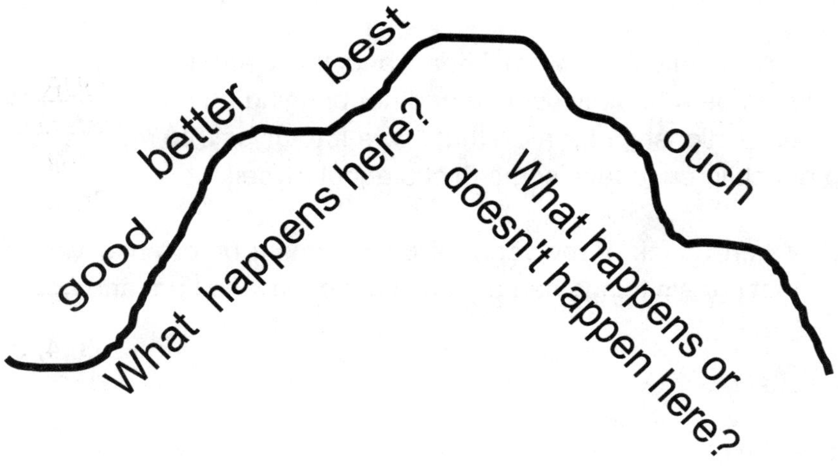
good
better
best
What happens here?
ouch
What happens or
doesn't happen here?

Personal Exercise: Ready for Marriage

As I reflect on what I read and think about being personally ready to be a healthy spouse and not bringing any "broken leg" traits to our relationship, I realize that I owe it to myself, to my spouse, and to our children to face some things about myself.

1. When I think of my years of development before marrying, I see that certain things had a major impact on *who* I am and *how* I am:

2. On a scale of 1 – 10, how would I rate my personal wellness for a healthy marriage?

3. Can I identify personal work I need to commit to?

4. Can I identify any ingredients for a healthy marriage I will commit to work on?

Couple's Exercise: Nurturing Our Marriage

1. What I need to do and stop doing to make you happy:

2. I know that you have the following needs:

3. I must admit some things about myself that get in my way of effectively and consistently taking care of you are:

4. Let's develop a prayer to say together regularly as a couple:

5. Let's renew or reword a wedding vow to reflect our current relationship and the love we hold for one another, and how we are committed to working together:

SPIRITUALITY OF COUPLE RELATIONSHIPS

Spirituality of Couple Relationships

"Do You Believe in Magic?"

That is the question asked in a love song from the 1960's. It is an interesting question to ask when pondering the spirituality of partners. Magic? The song said, "I'll tell you about the magic... It'll free your soul." We may not know for sure but if there is one spiritual quality that characterizes partner relationships, maybe it is not magic but surely it might be that of *mystery*. Have you ever wondered about why a couple gets together? What draws two persons together? What are the similarities and the differences that "two become one"? Often it is not something we can understand or maybe even see from the outside of the relationship. There is something mysterious, "magical", if you will, about partner relationships.

Some romantics may call it "magic". Some coming from a spiritual perspective may characterize what draws two persons together as "blessing". Magic or blessing there is some mysterious force that occurs when the spark of attraction develops to draw two persons to each other. Whether a relationship develops from that may depend on many things, the availability of the two persons, their age, their interest in becoming involved with another, curiosity, mutual values, just to name a few. Those many factors and how they play out is a dimension of the mystery. Why do some relationships grow and flourish and others simply start and end?

If a person finds themself in an exclusive loving relationship with another it is a precious gift. In the final moments of the play *Les Miserables* is the famous line that maybe says it best, "To love another person is to see the face of God". If we are blessed with someone to love and to love us, what kind of care should be given to such an opportunity? Someone once said to love and be loved by another person is the surest and truest way to work out our own salvation. Inside of a faithful commitment, to live in mutuality to serve the needs and happiness of another is to be offered one of life's great gifts.

To have this kind of commitment to another and from another is never to be taken for granted. More relationships die from neglect than abuse. A spiritual person would view the exclusive commitment to each other which blossoms from the spark of attraction as sacred. Many religious traditions characterize the commitment as a covenant. A covenant is a sacred promise, something beyond an agreement or a contract. When we commit to care and to love and to cherish another for a lifetime and ask others from the community to witness before God that commitment, it is a sacred act. Such a commitment between two persons is an occasion of grace. In the mystery of loving another in a sacred covenantal partnership is the opportunity not only to know blessings from God, but, in a unique way, to know the depth of love created by God.

It is to imitate God's care of the beloved and be the tender, sweet presence of God's love to the other. The ability to love beyond our own selfish needs is the grace of partner relationships. The journey of the partner relationship is, at the least, an invitation to create magic in life, in the sense of having the potential to become more than what one could ever become alone.

The good God must have had a vision of this before humanity could have lived it. Love invites us to grow beyond our self interests in the opportunity to serve the needs of the beloved. In the creation story, we learn of God's design to create, out of love, the human person. God could have easily stopped there. God could have left us on our own, a single person, to move through life being loved by God and loving God back. But what a plan! "No", God said, "I will make another, similar yet different, to allow my creature to know companionship of likenesses and differences in just the right measure. My creatures will have a beloved to learn of this great adventure to love another." God indeed created magic at that moment!

This is most readily seen in the witness of new love and in the great love stories in literature. To a lesser degree we see love between partners in a multitude of movies, books and love songs. If we are really fortunate, we have witnessed true love in our family and among our friends. If we are given an ultimate blessing, we have personally known the magic and mystery of love. Such love is celebrated with fanfare in most every culture in the covenantal marriage ceremony. A long marriage is considered one of life's great blessings. A loving lifelong partnership is one of the greatest joys that can be our delight in life. The spirituality of the path of partnership is to recognize the precious fragile gift we are given in our beloved.

Those blessed in partnership can never appreciate it deeply and reverently enough. If you are given the gift of companionship in a partner relationship treat it like the fragile reality it is. If another has made oneself available and vulnerable to you treasure that gift.

Anthony De Mello tells the story of God that I believe applies to marriage.

> *A woman dreamed she walked into a brand-new shop and, to her surprise, found God behind the counter. "What do you sell here?" she asked. "Everything your heart desires," said God. Hardly daring to believe what she was hearing, the woman decided to ask for the best things a human being could wish for. "I want peace of mind and love and happiness and wisdom and freedom from fear," she said. Then as an afterthought, she added, "Not just for me. For everyone on earth." God smiled, "I think you've got me wrong, my dear," he said. "We don't sell fruits here, only seeds."*
>
> *(Anthony De Mello, Taking Flight)*

If God gives you the seeds of the mystery that we call a partner to love, you may want to tend to that garden, with faithful devotion, and tender care.

Chapter Three

BUILDING A HEALTHY FAMILY

Building A Healthy Family

A family is a place
To cry and laugh
And vent frustration,
To ask for help
And tease and yell,
To be touched and
Hugged and smiled at.
A family is people
Who care when you are sad,
Who love you no matter what,
Who share your triumphs,
Who don't expect you to be perfect,
Just growing with honesty in your own decisions.
A family is a circle
Where we learn to think before we do,
Where we learn integrity and table manners and respect for other people,
Where we are special
Where we listen and are listened to,
Where we learn the rules of life
To prepare ourselves for the world.
The world is a place where anything can happen;
if we grow up in a loving family we are ready for the world.

(Christopher Gleeson SJ, David Lovell, A Canopy of Stars: Some Reflections for the Journey)

This description of what should happen in a healthy marriage is very thorough and filled with so many ingredients your family should think about and discuss. All of these ingredients take work to accomplish; they don't just happen. However, they are essential. They definitely can be accomplished. In fact, they must be accomplished. So, how is this done?

The relationship between parents and children should not be taken for granted. In fact, all the relationships within a family; parent to child, parent to parent, and sibling to sibling, require work in order for them to be nurturing, strong, and healthy. What is needed for these relationships to be good, productive, and effective is for all the people to consciously work on the various relationships. These relationships should not be taken for granted. The members of the family should not think wonderful, comfortable relationships will happen just because everyone ended up being in the same family. Whether a natural family or a blended family, if people want:

to truly be close
to feel comfortable and safe
to help each other build self-esteem
to appreciate one another
to cooperate in all that needs to be done
to enjoy one another's company
to make sure you have good memories
to want a relationship forever…

Everyone must be committed to the effort to make these things happen. This society of ours has many unhealthy messages that make parenting and raising children very difficult. There are so many messages parents must offset while teaching their children healthy values, attitudes, and morals they want them to have. Parents need to recognize what kind of work is in store for them, as parents, and for their children.

As you read this section of the book, it is going to be valuable to stop and check in with your children to see if they can relate and understand what is being suggested. Use examples that help children understand. For example, using metaphors can be very helpful. Children know and understand what it means for something to work as it is supposed to work. If they are into music, they know how their musical instrument is to work. They know how the group of musicians who are playing in a band or in an orchestra must work together to make the sounds come out as they would like them to. They want to make sure they are in harmony.

Children of all ages who are on athletic teams know what it is like to be in good shape to be ready to help the team. They know what it is like for a team to effectively work together. That wonderful term "teamwork" – ask them what it means, how it happens and if they value it? Every athlete knows the importance of working together, to truly be part of a team.

I am encouraging you to use examples that, in your family life, bring the subject matter clearly home to your children. With little ones, you might take a pencil and break it in half. This might help these children understand that there is something wrong with this pencil because it is broken. Because it is broken, it will be harder to use it for what it was made for. Any examples that help children know the difference between functioning effectively versus not functioning, being sick rather than healthy, of doing fine versus not doing fine are valuable. We want the children to understand that the family has to be a team. The family, like any other group of people, who come together as a team, must work together, must care about "winning," must have a good attitude, must at least make the right efforts, and be considerate of their teammates.

Each of the members who come to the team must be in pretty good shape and personally contribute to the team. If at times, it is obvious that something is wrong with the team, that something is broken down or not working quite right, then that means it is time to repair something, time for a team meeting. It is also important for each family member to be aware of their own personal wellness, motivation, and capability to work as a team member. Do you work together to fix the team as a unit? Do some persons on the team need to look at themselves and focus on their own personal wellness?

The family is the first and most important place for us to grow as we become ourselves. The family is one of the places where we will either be helped or hindered on this journey through life. The family is also critical in teaching us how to develop close, satisfying interpersonal relationships with others. Such things as positive self-esteem and confidence, our appreciation of people, communication and problem-solving skills, and our capacity for intimacy are just a few of those very important qualities that we must develop to be a whole healthy human being. The foundation for these life skills should start within our family life. Either positively or negatively, our family experiences establish a critical foundation on which our own personal life and our life with others will be influenced. The "movie of our life" starts with our family.

Let's focus on five specific ingredients for a healthy, effective, strong family. When these are present, both personal and interpersonal growth and wellness occur.

1. **Motivation:** Does it matter how we make each other feel?
2. **Relationship:** A real understanding and familiarity of one another so that the family members can claim to have a *relationship*, not just roles
3. **Expectations:** Clear and fair expectations everyone lives up to
4. **Effective Communication:** Solid communication and problem-solving skills
5. **Affection and Nurturing:** How we show love and appreciation for each other in our family

These are not listed in any order of importance because all five are very important. Share them with your family. Make sure each person understands them (at their own level of maturity) and then ask everyone to commit themselves *to living* the five ingredients. You don't want to just understand these ingredients; you want to live them!

1. Motivation

Motivation is best described as that attitude that says, "It matters to me to have a healthy home life and it matters to me how I make others feel." Consider having a family meeting discussing the following questions:

- Does it really matter to each one of us in this family how we make one another feel?
- Does it matter to you if we positively or negatively affect the self-confidence or the self-esteem of one another?
- Does it matter to the children if their siblings grow up liking themselves or not liking themselves?

- Does everyone in this family care if the members of this family like to be around one another?
- Does it matter to everyone that we feel safe and comfortable living at home together?

Obviously, for each one of these questions, there is really only one healthy answer! You may think some of these questions are pretty powerful, maybe too powerful to ask. They could stir up some anxiety in someone about whether or not you like them and care about them. Well, maybe some of that anxiety is important to develop and to let people get "stirred up." Maybe this is what gets people to take each other seriously and work together.

Far too often, family members treat one another in ways they would never treat a friend or colleague or someone they wanted to have like them. People in a family might take one another for granted. They might think that other family members do not appreciate them for what they do or who they are. There can be a general sense of wondering, "Does it matter to anyone around here what I am thinking, or if I am happy or unhappy or how they make me feel about myself?" Think about how important it is for family members to ask one another these questions. Family members should question how they *treat* one another, how they *talk to* one another; how they *make one another feel* about themselves.

No matter what answer you get, you will have something to talk about. If the answer is "yes", then you can talk about how everyone is willing to live it. You can talk about specific ways each person recognizes they could change. If the answer is "no", then you have a very clear, critical problem existing within the family. If the answer is, "I don't know," suggest that the person take some time and come back to it a little later because "I don't know" cannot be an acceptable answer. So whatever you get –"yes, no, or I don't know" - you have something you can work with. You have something you *must* work with. The reality is that everyone knows that the answers should be, "Yes, I care. Yes, my home life matters to me. Yes, my family matters to me."

What does it mean to have something to "work with?" Some examples might be:

A. Invite all the members of the family to write what they would consider a definition of a healthy effective, strong family.
B. How would each member of the family describe the kind of family they have?
C. What would each member say they could and would do differently to make the family a better place in which to live?
D. What would members suggest other members do differently to make it a better place in which to live?
E. If you have little ones who do not write, have them draw a picture of the family. Then have them tell a story about how the family is and how they would like it to be. Little ones have all sorts of insights and ideas about what should and should not happen in family life.

It is appropriate to expect people in a family to be able to identify what sort of things should happen in a family that make it a wonderful place to live. They can also identify those things that happen in a family that make it destructive, uneasy, hurtful, aggravating, and unsafe. They can ask themselves, "Does it matter enough to me to do something different? Does it matter to others? Will we work to make some changes?" It might be inspiring to post the words, "Does it matter?" around the house. It will raise a consciousness in everybody to be thinking about their level of motivation, how much it really matters to them to create a loving, safe, and caring family environment. It will enable everyone to compliment positive efforts and question negative behaviors. If you have some things happening in your home that are unhealthy, put some signs around to raise the consciousness to change these patterns. Get people to start thinking in terms of what matters, what is helpful, what is not helpful, and how they impact and influence the other people in the family. Expect everyone to become more and more motivated toward developing an environment where individuals can grow into healthy people and where each member of the family can enjoy living together and not be on edge over what will happen next. It should matter to everyone to create an environment that feels safe, kind, caring, and comfortable. This is what the ingredient of motivation is all about. "It matters! I care! I will show you it matters to me and I will work very hard with everyone."

How can we make motivation come alive? If we are motivated and truly care, if we are determined to show these, then what should the family do next?

Creating Family Contracts

1. Invite everyone to take some time and go somewhere in the house to think about what they would promise to do and promise not to do that would make a significant difference to the family. Everyone should think about how they might treat people differently or how they should talk to family members. What should they promise to do more often? What should they promise to stop doing? How could they each act differently so that their family time feels peaceful, comfortable, and wonderful? How can they create a family environment in which everyone wants to be there? Each family member should take time to think about these questions and come up with *specific* answers regarding their own personal behavior and the changes they will make.
2. The next step is to write these ideas down. Writing seems to insure deeper thinking and a greater sense of being organized. Writing also instills a greater sense of commitment. Once it's on paper, it somehow seems to reinforce a greater sense of reality – "I wrote it; I need to live it." It starts to feel like a contract, an obligation, a promise.
3. Now it's time to share. Wait until everyone is ready, even if it takes a few hours or days. It's important to give the message that everyone's input is important and expected. If someone refuses to participate, this is a serious problem; it may require getting professional help because it is so serious and so unacceptable. And, while professional help is sought, consequences should be exercised. If a person doesn't change what they need to because it's the right and healthy thing to do and because they care how they are

making someone feel, then some consequences that matter to them must be put into place. They must get the message, "If I don't change, then... will happen to me." The bottom line? Do not tolerate what is unacceptable and intolerable. Do not let someone be unhealthy and inappropriate.

Younger children may need help to formulate their thoughts and good intentions. Certainly suggestions can be made by a parent. The point is that everyone who is able to sense the concept of family should be included. Again, don't start until everyone is ready and *expect* everyone to get ready.

Once you're ready and together, turn off phones and televisions. It's time to focus as a family on what everyone is going to do to make this family a wonderful group of people to be part of.

If there are some family members who have some "unfinished business" between them that complicates their ability to work together, this may need to be addressed and resolved before creating the new contract. If creating the new family contract in itself is not enough to bring about some healing between these family members, then some sorrow, apologies, forgiveness, and willingness to move on may need to be done first. Again, the willingness to move on, to forgive, and to start over should be expected. Why shouldn't it? What other healthy option is there?

4. The family should now be ready to create the *Family Contract*. Write down each person's name. Each person tells the family what she or he will do or not do that will be good for the family. Their promise is written under their name. Once everyone has spoken and all the promises and good intentions have been written down, the contract is complete. Read the contract back to the family and make sure everyone agrees with what was written. Then everyone signs the contract. Make copies so everyone has their own personal copy to hang in their room.

Also, post the family contract somewhere in the house where people can readily see it on a daily basis. Agree that in about a week, a family meeting will be scheduled to see how everyone has been doing. Throughout the time until the next family meeting, use the contract to be aware of who should be complimented for their efforts or who should be reminded of where they may be falling short. With young children you may want to use stickers or happy faces to motivate and reward.

5. The family meeting is an opportunity for everyone to discuss how they see themselves living up to the promises they made and how everyone else sees each other living up to the contract. Notice how first it's a personal review and then an opportunity for everyone to give each other feedback. This process gives everyone a chance to practice showing that they care about how they make one another feel. This evaluation process should be done kindly, caringly, and non-defensively. Ideally, there are sincere compliments and statements of appreciation. If someone thinks a criticism is in order, how it's done will be very important. It's also important how it's received. If the person doesn't agree, it's still best to say something like "Okay, I'll pay more attention," or "I'll be more aware this next week." It's not easy to do, but it works better than arguing over who's right. Make sure everyone understands these guidelines for a family meeting and approaches the meeting with the right, most effective attitude. Here are some questions to get you started in your evaluation.

Self-Review: How I think I did this week…
What I hope you all noticed…
I found it easy or difficult to…
I'd like to ask _____ if she or he noticed…
What I intend to do better in this next week is…

Review of Someone Else:
What I was so happy to see was…

I noticed you did or didn't…and it was great to see…
I was disappointed when…
Would you be willing to …? to not … ?

6. Once everyone has had a chance to assess themselves and assess one another, it is time to decide what to do next.
   a) Should people continue to work on the same promise?
   b) Do people add another promise, while continuing to live the first promise?
   c) Does the past week's effort call for a reward or a consequence?
   d) Does anyone need some suggestions or advice?
   e) Can family members recommend changes to other family members?

7. In addition to spontaneous meetings or reactions, set the next scheduled family meeting. Identify what has been accomplished. Hopefully, the family has:
   - established how important motivation is and everyone is committed to being motivated
   - gotten specific on ways to prove each one's motivation by living differently
   - created ways to evaluate the levels of success and improvement
   - developed specific ways of rewarding and encouraging improvement and how to deal with someone who needs to improve with appropriate suggestions and possible consequences
   - started a precedent of working more effectively as a family and how to have successful family meetings

The first ingredient for a successful, healthy family – that everyone is motivated, that everyone cares – has been clearly identified and now you can work together to make it come alive and real in your family. Let's move on to the second ingredient.

2. Relationship

Relationship is when people truly know one another, respect one another, and care about how one another feels and thinks. Such relationships result in people feeling special, valued, and safe to share their own thoughts and feelings. Too often, families seem to just have roles they are living - parent, child, brother, sister, son, or daughter. There is a tremendous difference between having a role and having a relationship.

When we have a relationship, we truly know one another - what someone likes and dislikes, what makes them happy or sad, how they have fun, what they worry about, what their favorite activities are, what they pray for, and what they struggle with in daily life. In a good relationship, individuals want to know each other on a deeper, more personal basis and want to be there for one another. There is a difference between *having a relationship* and *having a role*.

It could be interesting to see how well you know one another by having some fun playing a quiz game together. You might call it, "How well do I know you?" or, "How well do you know me?" To play the game, start with something as superficial as one's favorite color, toy, or musical group and get a little deeper and more personal as the game proceeds.

Far too often in our families, it seems as though our conversations center around seven Cs: classes, chores, curfew, cost, computer, cell phone, and the car. Although the seven Cs are truly parts of our lives, they certainly don't lend themselves to a more personal, deeper understanding of and sensitivity to one another.

Take a survey of your family. Ask everyone to identify what topics seem to make up the majority of your conversations and discussions. What topics seem to take up the majority of your time together? Is there usually conflict and tension, or comfort and closeness? Do they result in knowing one another better and having a sense of being connected? Do you come away from these conversations and interactions feeling at peace and happy or upset and stressed out? The intention of this activity is to help you and your loved ones to get to a level of knowing and caring about one another in which you truly feel a closeness and a wonderful sense of comfort. How can we accomplish this?

First of all, find out if everyone wants to achieve closeness and comfort. Make sure everyone has this kind of motivation. Again, if some unfinished business or bad habits are already in the way, you want to get these out of the way either on your own or with someone's help. It will be important to get to an attitude of, "Let's agree that from now on we will...and we won't...so that building this closer relationship can happen."

The next step will be for everyone to share on a more personal level who you are and what's going on with you. Let's agree that mom and dad must do this first; the parents must set the example. As the adult, you may need to admit that you don't know how to do this very well, but you're willing to learn and to try. Such an open admission is wonderful. As a matter of fact, you already shared personally. You've already started.

You are hoping that as your children go through life that they will share with you, ask questions, and reach out to you when they're feeling challenged or bothered by something. You want to believe they will come to you. Now, why would someone do these if they don't feel close, if they don't feel like they really know you? What have they seen and heard you do with them as models for sharing and developing relationship?

- How often do you sit down and inform your children about what you've been doing? Do they hear you talk about the movie you saw or who you went with or what bothered you about someone? Make sure this is a sensitive sharing and teaching opportunity, not a "Let's talk about so and so" time.
- Do you share what you worry about? Do you talk about your own thoughts, feelings, joys, and concerns?
- Do you ask them questions like what they would do in your situation? Do you involve them in decision-making issues to get their input and ideas?
- Do you ever phone them and mention you've gone from one place to another or to say when you'll be home?

You hope that they will someday do these things. You hope they will talk with you in these ways. Think of the many things you are hoping they'll share with you, ask you about, and do for you. Are you doing these with them? Teach by demonstration, not just by words.

So, one of the ways I am suggesting you achieve the closeness and the relationship you want is to let others into your life, share your emotions and your thoughts. Share your feelings, talk about concerns, and let each other into hopes and wishes, likes and dislikes, fears and comforts, goals and dreams, and successes and discouragements. Let them know who's in your life and who's out or how an experience went and how you wish it would go next time. Take some time to think about such ideas as:

- What does it mean for someone to know me?
- What does it mean for me to know someone else?
- Sharing of feelings means…
- Being sensitive to one another means…
- Feeling safe with you means… With me means…
- Trust is when…
- "We can think differently and be ok" means…
- I want my children to trust me. Do they?
- I want my children to believe they can come to me. Do they?
- How do I let my children know me?
- When life gets complicated and difficult, I hope…
- Let's make sure we have fun together. How do we play together?
- Are there times you do things and don't do things just because you respect me and care how I feel? Do I do the same for you?
- Are there times we compromise with one another and work together?
- Let's agree to listen very carefully to one another and truly hear what we are saying, feeling, and needing.

Do you see what's happening here? These ideas, when shared, defined, and understood between two people result in what? A depth, a knowing, a caring, a respect, an importance, a bond, and a connection… a relationship happens!

When two or more people are only living roles with one another, it probably remains pretty functional and quite superficial. People can spend hours and hours, day after day, week after week, month after month, and really not know each other. Spending a lot of time around one another doesn't guarantee relationship. Even going through challenging times together – daily life, growing up, stages of life, tragic moments, and joyful times – doesn't guarantee relationship. Being born into the same family and sharing a bloodline and similar features do not guarantee relationship. All of these certainly create the opportunity for relationship, but they don't guarantee it. It's how we use them, how we truly do them together, how we talk and share, and how we let each other into our lives that determines if we have a truly deep relationship.

So, if having a meaningful, significant relationship is the goal, what is the equation to accomplish it? How about this:

Time for one another
+
having various experiences together
+
sharing thoughts and feelings
+
truly hearing and caring
+
treating one another lovingly
=
a wonderful, meaningful relationship

On your own and with significant others, evaluate how you are doing with each of the elements of the equation. How do you spend most of your time? What experiences happen between you? Do you share the thoughts and feelings you experience? Is there a sense of *knowing each other?* Do you make sure you understand and come across like you care? How do you express love and nurturing?

If building a wonderful relationship is important to you and others, then working at it is what you need to commit to. With the right motivation and efforts, people can accomplish this meaningful connection with one another. Limiting yourself to being superficial and just being functional can be raised to a wonderful level by knowing one another, being emotionally in-tune with each other, and feeling very content and pleased with how you treat one another. This is a healthy, wonderful relationship. This is connection. This is much more than just having a *role* with one another; this is having a *relationship*!

3. Expectations

The third element in family life is expectations. What do we expect of one another? What do I expect of you? What do you expect of me? Do we consider these expectations, appropriate, fair, and livable? And then, do we live up to these expectations and follow through?

Let me tell you about a meaningful family session that I was involved in as a therapist. The session involved a mother and father and three children. The session had become quite chaotic. There was yelling going on, people were crying, they were blaming each other, no one was listening, things were getting to the point where I could feel so much tension, pain and conflict that I started to wonder how this session could possibly pull together. Finally, the father, made the following comment. He said, "Wait a minute everybody. Kids, listen. Mom and I have never done this before. We have never been parents before having you kids, and we are trying to learn how to do a good job being your parents." Well, there was a tremendous silence. Everyone got choked up; the kids were stunned by the honesty of their father. The mom and dad, who had been sitting next to each other, reached out and held each other's hands. Both had tears in their eyes. Everyone sat there for a few minutes in silence and then the youngest child in the family said, "Well, I have never been a daughter before now either." That really helped. It broke the tension and caused the family to laugh for a moment, but the point was well made for everyone. Moms and dads frequently learn how to be parents by having children, and children learn how to be sons and daughters and brothers and sisters by doing this first-time run with the family they are born into. Everyone must acknowledge to one another that we are learning together. We learn to be parents, we learn to be children, and we learn to be sisters and brothers. Once this message was stated so honestly within the family, they began to work together at learning how to be a family, to be more what each other needed. They were now ready to talk about expectations and how to live up to them.

Everyone must be committed to this learning. Let's be patient at giving each other some time to learn what it means to be a close family. Understanding what each person is expecting of one another and finding out if everyone wants to live up to these expectations are important, critical issues to explore. Most arguments, frustrations, and hurts take place because someone is not doing what someone else is expecting. This might be happening because they didn't know what was expected or they didn't agree with what was expected. Whatever it is, it has something to do with expectations being broken down somewhere.

As such times, there is disappointment, hurt, frustration, anger. Notice the order I put these in. Frequently, I think people first get disappointed and hurt but jump quickly to frustration and anger. These last two are what are generally expressed. I believe people would be much more effective and accomplish more if they would gently express and show disappointment and hurt. Anger seems to lead the other to anger, and this interaction doesn't get people anywhere. If disappointment and hurt are shared appropriately, the people involved might be able to get somewhere together. Calmness and concern might replace upset and conflict. Pay attention the next time you sense your own frustration and anger, but control it. Calm down and see what happens if you express a sense of disappointment and hurt instead.

Another important point when thinking about living up to expectations is that this is the way people earn trust. When children reach a certain point in life where they want to be given additional privileges, such as driving the car, being given later curfews, or coming and going more independently, the issue will be if they earned the trust to be able to do these things. If they live up to expectations, trust will be developed. People should realize trust is not a birthright; it is earned. If lost, it must be re-earned. This is true for everyone. Parents earn trust, spouses earn trust, children earn trust, and siblings earn trust. Is everyone in the family committed to earning trust from one another? If so, everyone must agree on expectations and the importance of living up to them.

Another important point is that trust is not necessarily based upon age. Trust is established by living up to what is expected of you. For example, in deciding who you would trust to babysit your children, you recognize that there are some adults you wouldn't trust, but there are some teenagers you would trust. I remember when our sons were in high school, getting ready for prom and the prom parade. My sons and their friends asked if they could decorate and drive my car in the parade. I trusted them, and the answer was yes. It occurred to me that, there I was, trusting 17-year-old teenagers to drive my car. I knew some adults with whom I was nervous if they were even in the back seat. Trust is not age-based. This is an important lesson to teach your children. Sometimes, a younger child in a family makes it a point to behave in certain ways to gain trust in ways their older siblings didn't. Trusting has to do with the kind of person someone is. How much you respect them, have confidence in them, and trust them are determined by how successfully and consistently they live up to your expectations. Ask your children if they understand the significance of this. Do they understand its significance as far as their behavior and if they are to be respected, if people are going to be confident in them, and if people are going to trust them?

There are many times in life when living up to expectations is crucial for things to go as they should. We have expectations of how things should work or we repair them or return them. We have expectations of colleagues, teammates, people we hire, people we play music with, friends, etc. If expectations are lived up to, things go well. If not, we are hurt, disappointed, and aggravated. We all experience this on a daily basis in many ways. How well these expectations are met determines how we feel and how well life goes.

If you think about all the things and all the people in your life where living up to expectations is very important for your peace of mind, how much more important is the expectation issue for a family? It is obviously very important that moms and dads and children are all together on understanding:

- what is expected
- that expectations are fair and appropriate
- that everyone is committed to living up to them

What sort of an expectation list would you and your family create? Take some time to write one up. Everyone capable of writing and sharing expectations should put their own list together. Encourage the little ones to tell their expectations and someone write their list for them. The list should include what the family members expect of others and what they realize should be expected of them. How does your family's list compare with this one?

<u>Realistic Expectations for a Healthy Family</u>

We are kind and caring.
We show respect for each other.
Children obey their parents and do what they are asked to do.
We show responsibility without needing to be told.
We make good judgments that earn trust.
We know the *dos* and *don'ts* of healthy, moral living.
We communicate effectively with one another by listening, responding, and reaching agreements.
We problem solve effectively and avoid arguing.
We have relationships and closeness, not just roles.
We show affection and love and nurture one another.
We have impulse control. We don't always act like we feel.
We are clear on expectations and live up to them.
We express sorrow, we forgive, and grow from our mistakes.

So often in raising our children we find ourselves working harder than they are. The energies it takes to be on time, be responsible, or get homework done seem to be ours rather than theirs. Along with this disparity is their request to be treated as an adult and have material things that are apparently seen as birthrights rather than privileges and rewards that must be earned. Throughout your children's years of growth and development, be careful of reinforcing that certain privileges and rewards of life happen no matter how they might treat and talk to others. Let me give you an example.

If all day long your child has to be pushed to obey or his or her attitude and tone of voice are hurtful and disrespectful, then when it comes time to be driven to soccer practice, why would you say yes? Keep in mind – *if you don't react properly, then you are reinforcing.*

Children of all ages must learn that certain behaviors, attitudes, and comments result in certain reactions and consequences. If consequential thinking isn't developed in a person, their life will be characterized by irresponsibility, blaming others, and problematic consequences. This concept should be taught very early in life. There are numerous times when mom and dad should let a failure happen. Let something break, let an assignment not be turned in, let the child get an F, let the child miss a practice, etc. Then, as a parent, respond and react appropriately. Let the child experience whatever consequence comes from their decisions and choices. Obviously, I'm not talking about risking injury to oneself or to another – I'm talking about consequences that are safe and lead to valuable learning. A parent needs to be alert to how often their child's success is really because of what the parent did, not the child.

At some point, parent and child should know when it's time to back off and see how well they have learned the healthy moral and appropriate do's and don'ts of living life effectively. It's time to see what kind of independent young adult they are capable of being. The parents and child agree that life is now up to them. Unlike the growing up years, where parental intervention happens regularly, taking charge of one's own life and seeing how they manage should eventually be given over to the 17 or 18-year-old. Let these two years be a time for you to see how they handle everything. You and your child, this young adult child, should create the "personal expectations list," the list of things this young adult will now handle on their own, such as

Getting up for school
Deciding when I go to bed
Determining my curfew
Don't ask about homework
Getting to practices and to work
Completing home responsibilities
Putting gas in the car
Handling money

This is your last chance to observe how well they do while they're still living in your house. You can observe how mature and ready they are. If they prove they are not ready, you must intervene and react. This should lead to all sorts of work you will do as a family. However, if it isn't working, seek help. Bottom line – know your child's readiness for the challenges and decision-making responsibilities of life before they have moved out on their own.

Listen in on this session I had with Meg and her parents:

Me *Meg, as a seventeen-year-old, what is fair to expect of you?*

Meg *I don't know.*

Me *Meg, I hear you wanting your parents to back off and let you function independently and be able to have certain privileges. I'm trying to support you in these requests. So let's identify some responsibilities you're willing to live up to so that you are treated as a young adult.*

Meg *Okay, it's fair for them to expect me to get my homework done and improve my grades, to get myself up in the morning and be on time, to be pleasant at breakfast, but don't expect me to talk much. It's fair for them to expect me to ask for help if I need it on my schoolwork, and to treat people in my family nicely.*

Me *Mom and Dad, will you be able to leave the homework and grades up to Meg? (Remember, if it's your energy getting her through school, what will happen after high school when you're not around? Now is the time to find out if your son or daughter makes it or not. This is your last chance to find out how she will function while you are still around.)*

Parents *That makes sense.*

Me *Mom and Dad, will you be able to let her be on time or late, be okay with very little morning conversation, and observe how it goes with what Meg agreed to and respond with proper rewards or consequences?*

Parents *Yes.*

The values of this session are in how effectively and consistently the parents can become less active while letting the young adult sink or succeed. The parent must find some coping skills to deal with their worry, anger, sadness, wanting to take charge, and wanting to question. It will be very difficult to back off, especially if the history has been one of trying to control, yelling, pushing, getting angry, and doing things for the child.

Now, keep in mind that this example is of a seventeen-year-old. We must agree that at this age, whether truly mature enough or not, the young adult must be given the opportunity to be woken up as far as, "Whoa, look what I'm letting happen," or, "Look how well I'm doing when my parents back off and leave it up to me." I use this example of the seventeen-year-old because it gives us the opportunity to look at multiple valuable points in working as a family.

Becoming personally responsible should begin at early ages. Things like closing drawers, not dropping shoes on the stairs, putting things away, cleaning up the room, saying *please* and *thank you,* being kind, sharing, and putting the cap back on the toothpaste are appropriate behaviors to learn at different age levels. Making a list of what is appropriate to expect at each stage is an excellent idea.

However, making a list is not the most difficult task. How effectively Mom and Dad talk about the list, how gently and effectively they establish what it means to be responsible, how calmly they react when it's not going well, how capable they are of knowing when and when not to say something and how to say it, how well they practice what they preach… all of these need to be worked on by parents. For example, do you remember when I suggested learning to ask questions versus making statements? This is a crucial skill to learn. Questions must focus on being responsible, taking ownership, earning trust, and learning to take charge of one's own life. As parents, learn how to ask questions to get your children to think about the issues you want to lecture them on. I'm not suggesting you don't teach your children – on the contrary, it is your obligation! However, I am suggesting that at some point you must find ways to test how well they have learned. At some point, you go from teaching, what they might consider *lecturing,* to asking. Asking means they must think, and if you wait, they might come up with the right answers. Then you must find out if they *live* the right answers.

Overwhelmed parents don't do well at teaching responsibility. If you are struggling with some mental or emotional conflicts, if your world is overwhelming and weighing on you, you will bring this to your parenting role and will have trouble being effective. Overreacting or not reacting appropriately happens when we are not in a good place with ourselves. Be careful of this. If necessary, seek some help for these issues. We all need to know when the journey is too tough and overwhelming us. At such times, we shouldn't try to do it all alone. This brings up discussion on when medications are appropriate. We know that certain conditions like ADD, ADHD, and various emotional, mental, and behavioral problems can be treated with medications. With the help of approved medications, people can be more capable of learning new behaviors and controlling unhealthy, ineffective behaviors. I've always suggested people think of medications as either a crutch that needs to be used until the person is stronger or as a scientific blessing to help them function because their body needs it, similar to allergy meds.

Let's also look at the value of therapy. If mom, dad, and children find they are unable to accomplish what they need to on their own, then bringing in a pastoral counselor or a therapist as a member of the team for awhile becomes necessary. If we can't fix things on our own, we should get help. When we find the "rivers of the journey" rough, those moments, those relationships, those thoughts and feelings that seem overwhelming, these are times we may need two or more people to "paddle the canoe." We need to find partners to help us. This is when we need to reach out for help. We've all been there. We all get there. Don't let embarrassment stop you from getting the help you need. Remember Scott Peck's line, "Life is difficult?" Well, it is, and when living up to appropriate expectations of life gets to be too much, reach out! Trying to manage all alone isn't a good idea.

4. Effective Communication

Now we are going to focus on the fourth ingredient for healthy family life – effective communication. Earlier we talked about *what* families spend time talking about. In this chapter we are no longer focusing on the *whats* of conversation but rather on the *hows* of conversation. This chapter is on effective communication skills and effective problem-solving skills.

Someone cannot be on the basketball team if they cannot dribble. You can not be in the orchestra if you do not play an instrument. You cannot get a technology job if you do not know how to work with computers. Think of the hundreds of things people do where they are expected to know certain specific skills in order to participate in a particular activity or job. The expectation is taken for granted. People work at meeting the requirements so they can get a particular job or be in a particular activity or be on a specific team.

It should be expected, people should work at it, and people should hold one another accountable for effective communication skills. It is amazing how often in family life or in marriage what one is saying loses its value by the way they have said it. They have either explained themselves very poorly or they have allowed some of the non-verbals to contaminate their message so drastically that the entire point of what they were trying to say got lost. The message here is that a person might have a tremendously important point to make, but the point gets lost if they say it ineffectively. This happens very often in all kinds of relationships where people need to have good communication skills. There are some critical elements of good communication.

a. What do I want to say?
b. How can I best express this?
c. What words convey this as effectively as possible?
d. What tone of voice will be helpful?
e. Can I turn a statement into a question to promote discussion?

On the listening side:

a. Do I interrupt?
b. How well do I pay attention?
c. How carefully do I listen to what this person is saying?
d. Am I able to listen not only to what they are verbally saying, but the message they are conveying through their eyes, voice tone, and feelings?

Effective Communication is the combination of:

1. Verbal and non-verbal skills that result in expressing what you want to express
2. Listening and understanding
3. Responding verbally and emotionally so that people truly sense they are connected and have been heard

Let's look at each of these more closely. Ask yourself, "How am I doing in expressing myself, listening, and truly hearing and responding?" Everyone in the family should be asking themselves this same question. It's the combination of these skills that result in effective communication. Some of this material was covered earlier. However, in case you have chosen just to read the Family section, I want to make sure we cover this important topic thoroughly.

Verbal and Non-verbal Skills

Verbal skills are about using the right *words* to express the thought or feeling we're having in the most concise, clear way. Have you ever heard the statement, "Don't listen to what I'm saying; hear what I meant to say?" How often would this kind of communication work? Not very often! There may be some people in your life where you know them so well that there may be times when you know what they are trying to say. You have a sense of what they really want you to hear and understand. However, not only won't this work very often, you don't want to reinforce this kind of expectation. You should not allow people to get away with such a poor communication habit. Poor communication skills are learned and can be unlearned; good communication skills can be learned. People can learn the right words to express their thoughts and feelings in concise, clear ways. As a matter of fact, we should *expect* this learning of ourselves and others.

When effective verbal skills are compromised and people try to communicate without them, there are numerous negative consequences:

- Misunderstanding
- Frustration
- Anger
- Hurt feelings
- Confusion
- Not feeling connected
- Mistakes are made
- Distrust can build
- Failure to respond to and do what someone expected
- Someone thinks people don't seem to care what they're saying
- We fail to problem-solve, grow together, and make the progress we need to make

We certainly want to prevent all of these. None of us want any of those consequences. And yet, how often are they occurring in your family life? Too often? Then it's time for all of you to become committed to learning what works.

Tips for Effective Communication

1. <u>Think before you speak</u>. Speaking before thinking results in rambling, not saying what you want to say, sounding confused, and losing people's attention. Slow down and think out your message before speaking. Try to say what

you mean in as few words as possible and only once. Don't say the same message in a number of different ways. Think, make your point, convey your feeling, do it once, then stop and wait for a response. Notice the first step – think.

2. People can help one another with effective communication. People can prevent the negative consequences of poor communication with motivation to work together. How can people work together?
   a. Give one another permission to take time and to think through what they want people to understand and how they can say it.
   b. Agree to wait until people emotionally calm down. Our words and reactions can be influenced by our emotions. These emotions may be very appropriate and should be respected. However, we must ask ourselves if the message we want to give is going to be ruined by how we say it. If we had waited until we calmed down, would we have communicated more effectively?
   c. Don't ramble and don't snowball. Rambling is when you go on and on, repeating yourself, making your point in multiple ways and giving multiple examples. If you are still talking after a reasonable amount of time, you should probably suspect yourself of rambling. This is where the partnership agreement would help. If the listener would say, "I've got it," or, "I think I'm hearing what you want me to hear," and the speaker would accept this, rambling would stop and more effective communication could occur.

Another negative consequence that can accompany rambling is snowballing. Snowballing is the pattern of bringing up more and more issues. Each topic may be important and identifies something that is apparently bothering the speaker. However, it doesn't work to bring up so many topics at one time. It is like trying to play catch with two or more balls at one time. When someone throws too many "balls" at the other, effective communicating and problem-solving can't happen. Agree to stick to one concern at a time. There are several ways to prevent snowballing:

1. Specifically identify the topic, concern, or feeling you want to discuss.
2. Agree that if another topic or point is brought up, you'll accept the criticism that you've left the original topic and agree to back up.
3. Write down any new topics, concerns, or feelings being brought up so that you can revisit them some other time because they are apparently important. However, not now.
4. Agree that you must reach a solution, some sense of resolution, regarding your topic before leaving it, or, state very clearly that you're stopping it for now and will revisit it later. Then each of you must be committed to revisiting it, maybe even set a day and time.
5. Don't interrupt. Self-discipline is needed to listen and truly hear what is being said before commenting. Make sure the person is finished, not just taking a breath or pausing to think about how to complete their thought. It's even ok to ask, "Are you finished?" in a careful tone of voice.
6. Learn to ask questions. Sometimes the best way to make sure the person you're talking to listens to you and thinks about what you're saying is to *ask them a question*. Think about what you want to say, but convert it from a statement to a question and then be quiet and wait for a response. For example, instead of saying, "You really upset me when you…" change it to, "Do you know how you make me feel when you…?" or, "Does it matter to you what I'm saying?" Remember after you have asked a good question, be quiet. Don't follow it with, "because…" Doing this means you're about to explain why you asked your question. You're going to keep talking. This ruins the value and power of your question. Asking a question not only makes the other person listen and need to respond, it also promotes dialogue and conversation. Whenever possible, when you want to make a point, ask a question rather than making a statement.

7. Avoid responding defensively. This is probably one of the toughest things to learn. We so desperately want to defend ourselves, to correct what we think is incorrect and explain ourselves. However, this so often ends up being an argument over who is right or who is wrong. Think about the value of a very different response, maybe an apology or a sensitive comment that you care about how the person felt without worrying about who is right. For example, say, "I'm sorry you took it that way," or, "I'll try very hard not to have you feel that way again," or, "I'll try to do it better next time." Notice that in these responses, you're not agreeing with nor disagreeing or challenging what the other person said; you're just showing concern about how they felt and that you want to move on. It doesn't become an argument over who's right or wrong. The focus stays on how the one person interpreted something and how they felt about it. Taking care of these reactions is more important than defending or being right. Healthy responses focus on being *concerned* versus being *right*.

When a family is sitting around the dinner table and someone has a very sour face, someone might say, "Hey, is something bothering you?" If that person answers *no* in a tone that says *yes* they have actually said a great deal. They have said something is wrong. Sometimes that person may not respond at all. Why would we allow someone to get away with this kind of response? We would not allow it anywhere else. It would not work at work or if you are on a committee. No coach is going to allow it of a team player, and no band leader is going to let a person get away with no response. Far too often we accept and allow in our family relationships what we would not allow anywhere else! The obvious point is, let's not allow in our family life what we would not allow anywhere else. Let's hold one another accountable for responding, for our tone of voice, our volume, our facial expressions, and our body language because all of these things influence the message.

There are several other effective communication methods. One is to write what is difficult to say. We can bring up sensitive issues in writing - *Dear So and So, I have been having trouble with something that I would like to share with you and maybe we can communicate on it for a while through the mail then maybe someday talk.* If we find it hard to express love and admiration, we can write that in a letter - *Dear So and So, I have been thinking lately how much you mean to me and I have wanted to tell you this and I am going to tell it to you in a letter.* Someone who gets a letter like this is probably going to hang onto it for the rest of their life. So often we let things go unsaid because of difficulty with personal communication. Writing a note or sending a letter or meaningful card can be very effective.

Another way to communicate can be by phone, especially in parent-child relationships. It might work out very well to break the ice a little bit on a particular topic by trying to talk about it on the phone. Using a cell phone or texting are possible ways to start to address a difficult topic or to communicate something you have wanted to say directly. Methods like these might initially make it easier to get a conversation started.

Another excellent vehicle for communicating is a family meeting. Be careful not to make family meetings something you do only when there is a problem. The children might begin to think family meetings happen only when something is wrong. I think it is important to establish that people have family meetings for all kinds of reasons. They get together to talk about how well things are going, to make some plans for the weekend, to plan a trip, or to share a concern someone is having. Families get together to work out something that is going wrong and needs to change, as well as when things are going very well or it's time to plan family fun.

Another factor in effective communication is timing. One of the best times to talk to children is at bedtime, when they have gotten into their pajamas and are ready to be tucked into bed. They understand you are setting aside this time just to be with them.

What can we do if a particular member of the family refuses to talk? Refusing to communicate is not acceptable. It's time to expect appropriate behavior that not only contributes to the family, but indicates the individual is healthy and mature. Obviously, we would hope that the necessary changes would happen because the person cared and was motivated by the relationships in the family. However, when this motivation is missing, then rewards, privileges, and consequences must come into play.

If these motivators don't work and the individual continues to demonstrate non-communication, then individual and family therapy should be considered. More often than not, the efforts eventually prove worthwhile, as long as everyone follows through with the treatment plan, both in sessions, as well as at home. If the individual pushes the limits and remains oppositional, forcing the family to consider hospitalization or legal intervention, you are then in crisis mode. The parents and therapist will need to work very closely together to plan the next steps. This is not typical, but unfortunately, needs to happen more often than we would hope.

Is it fair to expect people in a family to communicate? Should we expect people to resolve issues? Should we expect people to care how they make one another feel by their silence or by their refusal to explain what is going on? Absolutely! The expectation to grow together should be made. If the effort does not result in the person being able to change on their own, then they should get some help to change it. Do not accept it. It has to be established that these expectations are critical, and as soon as you compromise them and give in to them, you are setting the precedent for some very serious problems. Remember, *if you don't react, you reinforce*. If communication is absent and you cannot fix it on your own, seek help. Do not settle for broken, ineffective communication patterns. Expect effective communication. Expect appropriate behavior. Seek help to get them. Don't stop the help until the patterns are consistent and you can claim to have good communication, effective problem-solving skills, and behaviors that make for a healthy family.

5. Affection and Nurturing

This brings us to the fifth element – the importance of affection and nurturing. The child within each of us continues to have emotional needs no matter how old we get. In many ways, what we needed when we were two or three years old continues to be present throughout our life. We all have the need to be touched, held, and told how special we are. We all like to hear, *Thank you, I appreciate what you did, I missed you, I'm sorry,* and *I love you*. These words, if sincere, truly meet our emotional need for nurturing.

Any time we are deprived of affection, nurturing, and loving messages, the consequences are emotional pain. Emotions such as sadness, loneliness, emptiness, anger, frustration, and depression are some painful feelings we can experience. Affection and nurturing, and the many ways these can be expressed, are as crucial to our well-being as water, food, and air.

It would be valuable for you as a family to open up and to talk about showing affection and nurturing. Don't think that the only form of affection has to be something physical, like a hug or a kiss. Although that kind of affection is special and very important, realize there are other ways people can show affection. A facial expression, a smile, a nod, or a pat-on-the-shoulder, are wonderful behaviors people can do to demonstrate affection. Refer to Gary Chapman's *Five Love Languages* for further details. The point is to have ways in which you show affection to one another. For some people these behaviors may not come naturally, but since they are so important to our overall health and happiness, people should work to make them part of their lives.

If someone was raised in a family in which behaviors of affection were absent, they will not know how to demonstrate these behaviors. Expressive behaviors will feel foreign to this person. They might feel awkward, clumsy, and embarrassed to give hugs, kisses, or touches on the shoulder. Even enthusiastic compliments may seem like a new language that they never learned. It's important to understand that all new behaviors start out feeling uncomfortable, but, if we stay with them, they can eventually feel better and better. Keep in mind that just because a behavior takes effort, it doesn't mean that it isn't sincere. As a matter of fact, there is something very special and lovingly wonderful when a person cares enough about someone else to make the effort to learn new behaviors that the other person wants and needs.

How does your family show love and affection? How do the members of your family get messages from the other members that they are special, loved, valued, and appreciated? Sit around together and ask these questions. Does each family member think they express affection and nurturing often enough? Do they think they receive affection and nurturing often enough? Does everyone in the family truly care about everyone's answers? And finally, is everyone motivated to increase the behaviors of showing affection, nurturing, love, and appreciation?

Sometimes we can understand that someone loves, values, and appreciates us, but the person is limited in their ability to express it, and we have to accept this and be content. The point of this chapter is to make sure the members of a family go beyond just knowing and believing and decide to learn to express and show affection, appreciation, and love.

What specific behaviors of affection, nurturing, loving, and appreciating are we talking about?

Verbal (speaking or writing one's own written messages or the writings of others)

- I love you
- I like you
- I appreciate you
- Thank you
- What can I do for you?
- You are special to me
- Have I told you lately…
- I feel blessed that you are in my life
- I'm sorry
- I didn't mean that
- I won't say or do that again
- I forgive you
- You're beautiful
- What a wonderful job you did
- I like how you …
- I am so glad that you are in my life

Non-Verbal

- A hug, a kiss
- Holding hands
- Sitting beside each other

- A touch
- Rubbing the neck
- Arm around the shoulder
- Sitting on your lap
- Lying beside each other
- Gently touching someone's face
- Rubbing the back
- Hand on the knee
- Rubbing the head
- Brushing the hair

Studies have been done that demonstrate the human need for touch, affection and nurturing. When these needs are met, people are happier, have stronger self-esteem, demonstrate more energy, and are physically healthier. We absolutely need these. Without them, we become negatively affected, both emotionally and physically. With them we are positively affected. These are crucial concepts for your family to be aware of and to be committed to doing something about. Make sure these expressions of affection, nurturing, and valuing are included in your *Family Contract*. Talk about how important it is for each of you to receive nurturing because it does so much for your happiness and daily energy. Also help each person to recognize how learning to nurture and show affection will be valuable to them the rest of their life in all the relationships they will have.

The Life Changers

It is critical to help your children understand the life changers and be committed to developing safe habits with them in their daily lives. The life changers are:

- Drugs
- Alcohol
- Sex
- Cars
- A legal record
- Use of the internet, Facebook …

Can you think of any you would add to this list? In these critical areas of life, parents and children need to discuss:

- What will you do when…?
- How will you handle it if …?
- Can you understand that if you … it becomes more difficult to stop?
- What do you think will happen to you if you …?
- Does it matter to you if …?
- Can I count on you to …?
- Let's agree that if you're in a situation like …, you'll call me.
- What secret code names or code sentences should we use when you need to be picked up?

Blended Family

Before moving on to the family exercises, let's discuss some unique challenges for the blended family. In addition to everything that has been said regarding family wellness, the blended family needs to consider specific challenges that come with bringing two families together or in bringing a new person to the family. How can we develop a healthy blended family? Far too often in blended families – a second marriage in which one or both partners have children from previous relationships – I hear such language as "your kids; my kids; you're too easy on them; you're too hard on them; or we agree on expectations but you don't follow through." Theoretically, you can recognize that none of these statements will effectively work well in family life. What attitudes should be present?

Efforts should be made so the natural parents and stepparents all give the message, "We are working together as co-parents in raising *our* kids." This will mean that, as often as possible, all the parents in both homes have similar expectations, rules, rewards, and consequences. It means all the parents communicate with and support one another. This may take a lot of work, especially after divorce. It may even require some therapy to accomplish such teamwork. For the emotional, mental, and behavioral health and development of the children, this teamwork is crucial. If the three or four adults work together as co-parents, not only will their lives go more easily and be less complicated and frustrating, but the children will also do much better. Most often, the children will test these co-parents, trying to manipulate and cause some confusion. They may even use the trump card, "If you don't let me have my way, I'll go live with my other parent." This should never be given into! The children, somewhere inside themselves, know they shouldn't get away with such threats and manipulation. They need you as co-parents to be working together and similarly.

"I'm not their mother or father." This is obviously true. However, whoever is in the children's lives functioning in a parental role is to be seen as "Mom" or "Dad." The children may not call you "Mom" or "Dad," but the adult's mentality should be one of functioning as a mom or dad parent. As co-parents, it's important to work on:

- developing a meaningful relationship with all the children
- being seen as a parental teacher
- participating in the children's lives and attending their activities
- watching for and making opportunities to be loving, affectionate, and nurturing
- expecting all your children to respect, listen, and be responsive to the efforts of the adults as parents
- following through consistently with what you say will be rewards or consequences

- discussing with the children what kind of relationship they would like to see develop between themselves and the stepparent

Children should not feel guilty or frustrated for loving or caring for someone like a parent or stepparent. If this love is seen by the other parent as a betrayal or rejection, then the child is not free to make choices. The child should never get the message that they must pick sides. Unless some very clear and drastic unhealthiness is truly present, this should never become the conflict for a child. However, if it is the reality that a parent is struggling with some serious, handicapping problem, such as alcoholism, addictions, major depression, severe anger management issues, then the child will need to have a pastoral counselor or therapist help them to understand this and figure out healthy ways to deal with this reality. This is a crucial issue for divorced parents and blended family parents to pay attention to and act responsibly regarding it. This kind of decision-making regarding a parent must be done with kindness, caring and some objectivity that can come by using a professional.

Tips for Divorced Spouses
Who Should Continue to be Effective Parents

Two people who have decided not to live together should still be effective co-parents. What is important to a child is to be able to believe that <u>both</u> parents:

1. Will continue to love me
2. Will remain in my life, and
3. Will work together for my sake

I understand how often two divorcing people have serious negative thoughts and feelings about one another. Hurts, angers, resentments, and various criticisms make working together difficult. One of the spouses could truly be the main reason for why the marriage is ending. Far too often, a well-intentioned parent questions being able to count on the efforts of the other parent. All these factors make the journey during and after divorce all the harder for everyone, including the children. For the children, the mental, emotional, and behavioral consequences can become devastating. You, as parents, can prevent this. It will mean handling some of your feelings, beliefs, and concerns, at least for now, in constructive ways.

I hope you are moved to consider what your children need from you. Even though healing the marital relationship did not happen, you can and should put efforts into healing the parental relationship and making it effective for the sake of your children.

Probably the most difficult issues to handle will be your personal conviction that:

- My ex was at fault;
- My ex treated me terribly; and
- My ex is a poor example for and a negative influence on our children.

As true as these may be, I encourage you to be very careful what you do about these beliefs. So many of these tips are important and critical for all children. However, some are age-based or "ready-for" based. Parents must be sensitive to this timing and sense what a child can and cannot handle and what they're ready for.

1. Assure your children that the divorce is not because of them.
2. Younger children need to be reassured that they will be taken care of and that other major changes (home, school, neighborhood) will try to be prevented if possible.
3. Create frequent and consistent times for the children to be with each parent. Parents should remain reliable and consistent. When you are with your children, be affectionate and loving. Don't overdo activities and entertaining the children. Work at developing a consistent home life in both homes.
4. Show your children a great deal of warmth and affection. A child can worry that, since you stopped loving one another, maybe you might stop loving them. Children may question the stability and reliability of love.
5. Don't let the children witness too much of your emotional upset and pain. While worrying about how to take care of their parent, they may hide their own emotional pains and

upsetting thoughts because they sense that their parent just can't cope with another concern.

6. Children will need permission and help to express their thoughts and emotions. They need to release these and to learn how to do so appropriately.
7. Don't argue in front of your children or where you can be heard. Delay touchy topics and difficult times for the sake of your children.
8. Avoid criticisms, demeaning statements, and name-calling. Be conscious of your voice tone and other non-verbal expressions. Spare children from having to deal with such negatives, from having to pick sides, and from thinking they're expected to be critical of the other parent.
9. Never imply that a child's time with the other parent is punishment. For example, don't say, "If you act like that I'll send you back to …" Never let yourself be threatened by a child saying, If you don't let me … I'll go live with…"
10. Encourage your children to include the other parent in their life and in significant events. Phone calls, invitations, and sharing of accomplishments should be encouraged by both parents.
11. Make sure the children have no sense of obligation or responsibility to rekindle the relationship or to save the marriage. Help them to give up their hope that their parents will return to marriage.
12. Talk about their hopes and dreams that their parents could be happy together. Let them know that it didn't work and it won't happen. Lead them into the tasks of acceptance and moving on.
13. Don't convey the message, directly or indirectly, that you are upset and feel betrayed by the child's wanting to be with the other parent. Make it safe for the child to care about both parents.
14. Don't put your child in a spying, tell-on-the-other position. Don't ask them to be the messenger for some topic you're uneasy talking with your ex about.

15. As many rules, expectations, morals/values, priorities, rewards, and consequences that the parents can agree on, the healthier it is for the children. This will also make parenting easier for Mom and Dad.
16. Have your children understand that major decisions require both parents' participation: schools, medical issues, financial responsibilities, driving the car…
17. Delay dating until your children are ready. Preparing your child for this "getting on with your life" is very important but shouldn't start until other adjustments have been accomplished.
18. If another person was part of your life before the divorce, I would encourage you to put this relationship on hold for months. The adjustment to the divorce gets very complicated by this person's presence.
19. Older, more mature children may need to deal with the reality that their parents live life differently and may need to choose which lifestyle is best for them. Parents will need to be able to discuss this choice and to evaluate it with their children reasonably and calmly. For example, religion, worship, moral differences, priority differences, attitudes about various topics may all be areas of life in which the parents have differences. Often times, these are some of the reasons the marriage didn't work. As each of the parents live their lives, the children will ultimately need to decide which practices and attitudes fit them best as they move on with their own lives.
20. If the children had good relationships with extended family, make sure these relationships continue.
21. Notify significant others, such as teachers, counselors, ministers and coaches about what is going on in the child's life. Ask for their help in watching for signs that the child may be struggling. Give them permission to talk with your child about how he or she is doing.

Ideally, these suggestions make sense to you and your co-parent and both of you are committed to the efforts. If you find yourselves having difficulties, seek professional help and maybe even include the children. If you have an uncooperative ex who is not willing to work with you in co-parenting effectively, then consider getting help for yourself and your children. Whether alone or with your co-parent, whatever efforts you make will be beneficial for you and your children.

Family Exercise: Five Ingredients for a Healthy Family

1 - Motivation – it matters how we make each other feel

1. What would family members list as important to them in their lives?

2. Where does the family fit into each person's list of what's important?

3. Where do the feelings of each family member fit into the priority lists?

Once again, if it matters to everyone in our family how we make one another think about themselves and feel:

- What behaviors or statements should continue?
- What behaviors or statements should stop?
- What behaviors or statements should start?

2 - Relationship

1. What is the difference between having a *relationship* with someone and having a *role* in their life?

2. Think of someone in your family you would want a better, closer relationship with.

3. What would need to happen?

4. What would you need to say? To share? To ask? To talk about to become closer?

5. What would you need to do more often? What would you need to stop?

6. What attitude would you need to develop about closeness and having a meaningful relationship?

3 - Expectations

Very often, what gets in the way of satisfying relationships is when someone fails to live up to what someone else expected. Think about this for a few minutes. When you are upset with someone, hurt, angry, frustrated, or confused, or they are upset with you, what happened or didn't happen? Probably you expected some behavior, statement, tone of voice, or reaction that didn't happen. Or something did happen that was just the very opposite of what you wanted and expected. The same disappointment and frustration is true for the other person as well.

1. As a family, get more specific. Think about specific people in your family and what expectations you would want to be able to count on from now on?

   Behaviors…

   Language…

   Voice tones…

   Responsibility…

What would these same people want to be able to expect of you?

2. What are the most frequent upsets in your family? What arguments seem to happen most often? What expectations are not lived up to? What failed expectation causes this argument, hurt, anger, or upset?

3. What can you agree to do or not do from now on? What promises can be made?

4. Does any specific expectation seem unfair or overwhelming to anyone? Should it be? If not, then someone must grow and change so that they live up to this expectation. If yes, it is unfair and overwhelming, then someone must change their expectation to be more realistic and appropriate.

5. What expectations do you have for your children to show responsibility at their ages?

6. Are you and your children ready to increase expectations, to provide opportunities to earn respect and trust, and to reach a level of healthy interdependence?

4 - Communication Skills

1. Good, effective communication is when…

2. In order to accomplish this effective communication, people must…

3. How is your family doing with these? Are people:
   - saying what they want to say?
   - listening?
   - responding or not responding?
   - aware of voice tone?
   - aware of inappropriate silence?
   - failing to initiate?
   - talking too much or not enough?
   - rambling?
   - repeating?
   - interrupting?
   - paying attention to feelings and emotions?
   - snowballing?
   - learning to revisit so that there is no unfinished business?

4. What specific communication skills do you need to learn and to work at? What would others want you to learn to do and not do?

5. What skills do you want members of your family to learn to do and not do?

6. Find out if everyone is committed to the agreement to always resolve issues, either at the moment or within a reasonable period of time. What does resolve mean to each of you? Can you agree that it means to reach the same agreement, or to be able to compromise, and to be willing to revisit it if some resolution wasn't accomplished?

5 - Affection and Nurturing

Talk about how you express love, affection, and nurturing in your family.

1. Do each of you think you express it often enough?

2. Do each of you think you receive enough love, affection, nurturing, and affirming?

3. What specific verbal and non-verbal ways of showing affection do you agree should happen more often?

4. Talk about why expressing love and affection is important now and in the future. What makes it difficult for you to express this?

SPIRITUALITY OF FAMILY

Spirituality of Family

Family: The School of Love

Family is the foundation of so much spiritually in our lives. If all goes well in families it can be like the gift of having clean air to breathe. It is vital to our well-being but it is the type of gift one can take for granted. Growing up in a healthy, solid, loving family is a sure sign of God's presence to a child. Our image of God and the experience of trust that develops in our family of origin is the foundation of an experience of faith. Our perception, of God the giver of life and source of love, is grounded in the daily experiences of family life: being fed, being clothed, being bathed, and being comforted. Beginning life in an attentive family is hopefully where one learns to experience God's love through the care given by parents. This original experience of love and trust can wrap a person in safety, comfort and peace, It is almost an invisible shelter, a harbor against the trials and challenges that we bump into in the world as we move through life.

Spiritual Practices in Family Life

The invisible gift of a loving family can help us to avoid sleepwalking through this journey of life. Recently I was told about a conversation between two young adults, a brother and sister, who are doing well in their initial independent stage of life but who have not yet settled into the BIG decisions like who to marry, where to live, what job to settle into. As they discussed "life" they acknowledged the unsettledness of their lives and they realized they shared something else… a confidence and sense of purpose and optimism that God's plan would unfold in their lives and, in time, their future will work itself out as it should for them.

Knowing these young people, I have no doubt they know their lives will include disappointment, challenges and struggle. They know there are bumps in the road, even heartache and sometimes heartbreak. While they don't focus on the difficulties, they realize challenges will be part of their lives. And yet somehow in a deep, important and sacred place they know God holds them and will forever. They don't know everything, but they know through all of the unknowns of the future... they have faith, a faith that God has a personal interest in them and a unique plan for them.

But being young adults ahead of the curve... they wondered where that ultimate trust they bravely carried into independence came from. As I listened to them I heard as they reflected, maybe to their surprise, that they realized their Mom and Dad had bequeathed that trust to them in a thousand ways through the faith they had passed on to them. They had watched through their child's eyes the way Mom and Dad had trusted God through job changes and job losses. They had a witnessed the joys of family gatherings, the challenges of moves and disappointments and saw their parents staying close to a faith community through it all. They gave to and took solace from those people of faith who surrounded them. From them and from their family and friends they had observed what had sustained their parents through the good and bad times.

This young man and young woman had the inheritance that comes from a family that practiced consistent worship, gave them a foundation of knowing their faith tradition, showed them evidence of the generosity of God's love by serving others. They move into their own lives with a hope and trust in God's plan and purpose. They concluded it was passed down to them from their Mom and Dad.

Isn't that what all parents long for our children, to take in the backpack of their heart when they move out on their own? I don't believe there is one moment when that happens. It comes from a lifetime of moments as your children watch how you live and respond to life, even and maybe especially, when life throws you a curve ball.

When we are preparing parents for the Baptism of their children, we share a lovely poem with which you may be familiar. In it we are reminded of what we teach through our daily actions... whether we are conscious of it or not:

> When you thought I wasn't looking, I saw you
> made my favorite cake for me and I learned little
> things can be the special things in life.

When you thought I wasn't looking I heard you say
a prayer and I knew there is a God I can talk to
and I learned to trust in God.

When you thought I wasn't looking I saw you make
a meal for a friend who was sick and I learned that
we all have to help take care of each other.

When you thought I wasn't looking, I saw you give
your time and money to people who had nothing
and I learned that those who have something
should give to those who don't.

When you thought I wasn't looking I felt you kiss
me good night and I felt loved and safe.

When you thought I wasn't looking, I learned most
of life's lessons that I need to know to be a good
and productive person when I grow up.

(Author Unknown)

These are the moments we can focus on as parents, the thousand moments when we don't think our children are looking, but they are looking. By watching how parents live, children learn what faith in God and resiliency in life means.

Consider this moment in your family's life? What is God teaching and revealing to you in this time? This moment in your family's life will never come again. Once in a lifetime, your child, is five weeks old, three years old, twelve years old, sixteen years old. This season of this year will never come again in his or her life. What is God saying to you at this moment in time? What in this moment of time is God saying to you and to your family? Each day is a new beginning of a new year, a new cycle of listening to God and learning in the family, *the school of love*.

The Practice of Gratitude

My daughter-in-law was prompting my granddaughter to use the special word she has been working on to express waiting uncomplainingly when things take longer than expected. She asked Maria, who was three years old at the time, what was that special word? Maria, answered, "Thank you." Well…"Patience" was the word Mom was looking for but we both had to smile…

You may have thought about gratitude as a noun. I am suggesting you consider its value in life as a verb. It can be a life practice to consciously and continually adopt an attitude of gratefulness for life, in general, and for individual moments and experiences of life, in particular. This takes practice. A snowfall, a sunrise, a smile, a compliment, a warm breakfast, a healthy body, a friend, a favor, a good leader… the list is endless if you think about it. We all can take so much for granted! It often is a matter of what we choose to focus on in life. Do we focus on the minor irritations and inconveniences or on the beauty and opportunity in front of us? Do we focus on this graced season of our family or does it slip past us without notice or appreciation? Adopt the attitude of gratitude and see how much more deeply your spiritual life develops.

Faith is a gift from God passed to us from others, usually through family and a faith community that we can personally cultivate or ignore. If we want to pass on the gift of faith to our children the most important thing we can do is nurture our own faith. If you want your children to believe and to live the gift of faith you must cultivate a faithful life yourself.

I'm not sure we can give "faith" but we can model it and witness to it. We are able to teach a religious tradition and cultivate an appreciation for our spiritual nature. We have a bodily reality, an intellectual reality, an emotional reality and a spiritual reality. Our spiritual reality is something we have to learn to appreciate. We will not know a religious tradition without being taught its beliefs, language and practices. To pass a faith on to our children we must live what we say we believe. As we become aware of our spiritual reality, we learn to see with the lens of faith.

As a child, I had very poor eyesight but it was not flagged until I was about in fourth grade when I was given my first pair of eyeglasses. It was fall and I remember walking home from the eye doctor who lived just down the street and being awed by the individual leaves on the trees! I had no idea you could see each leaf up so high from the street! I finally had a lens to see something that was always there but I was not able to perceive. To see through "another lens" is an analogy for the gift of faith. God's presence and grace is always there but only with the lens of faith can we see it. This is the spiritual lens you may hope to have to guide you in life. This lens can be a spiritual benefit to you and something you can pass on to your family.

Another possible way to vision this gift of faith is that it is "a treasure" you may possess and that you wish to pass on to your children. Sometimes people find it helpful to image this as something concrete. One such image is to picture a classic "hope chest". Generations ago a family would give a child a "hope chest". Throughout the child's life the family would put things in it, linens, blankets, mementoes, valuables, holiday and religious objects. The idea was that whenever that child left the family they took this chest with them and what they had been given was theirs, the blankets to warm and comfort them, the linens to bring social grace to their lives, the mementos to bring back meanings and memories of the family one came from.

This is an excellent image for passing on the gift of faith. In fact, some churches actually create literal chests for their children to be given at Baptism and the baptismal garment and other religious objects are collected in the "Faith Chest". It is really a lovely way to keep all the resources for nurturing faith at various milestones of a child's life. The "Faith Chest" and its contents are resources the child has to see and to take when with them when he or she is grown or leaves home.

Whether you create an actual chest or not you may find this image useful to imagine each of your children as having a kind of a hope chest of faith *in their heart*. It is invisible but you as the parent are "placing in your child's heart, experiences, celebrations, emotional attachments, memories, conversations, experiences of serving others and various devotional practices.

This is a good image because these are treasures that may help us in childhood and adolescence. However, at the time, perhaps these gifts don't seem as valuable as material gifts, nor even some great life experiences, like travel. They may not give us as much in status or achievement like sports, academics or other activities. But they may be the gifts that sustain your child in ways and times when they need something the most and the world can't help them. The wisdom of a religious tradition, faith and an appreciation for our spiritual nature can be the resources that get us through sickness, suffering, or loss. It can be the way we understand the meaning in our life and interpret the experiences we have in a purposeful way.

The greatest thing we put in our child's "Hope Chest of Faith" and in their heart is the gift of love. Your home is, to quote a Catholic Church document, "the school of love". It is the place where we are educated in how and why to "love". Through experiences in your family your child's treasure chest will become filled with your love which is the foundation on which all other relationships are built. I believe, the most effective way a child can come to know God and develop a relationship with God is, for you as a family, to engage and be faithful to a religious tradition. Faith ultimately is cultivated within a family and in a community. Through the gift of faith a person learns to talk, to listen and to trust God. In that relationship with God a person has a presence to guide them, to teach them... to love them. To nurture your child into a relationship with God is the gift of a lifetime. In that relationship they will come to know, no matter what happens in life, they will never go through it alone. The Lord is with them in the best and in the worst of times.

Ultimately faith and love are gifts that are at the core of our beliefs and what animates the values we live by. What are the values that you treasure and want to pass on to your children? What are the beliefs you hope your child lives by? The opportunity a family has to change the world through passing on these gifts is simply awesome. Take some time to think about what you would like your children to hold onto after you are not there to "hold their hand" in life. Knowing what you want to leave them in the "Faith Chest" of their hearts is the first and most important step on that journey.

The Practice of Prayer

Prayer is obviously a core practice to develop a spiritual atmosphere within a family. Prayer can mean many different things to different people. What are some ways you can pray as a family? Two basic ways of praying are *spontaneous prayer and rote prayer.*

Spontaneous Prayer

Spontaneous Prayer is prayer that one speaks out loud or silently that is conversational in nature. This, too, is a practice that is easily integrated in the relationship between a parent and child in simple everyday ways. In our home we prayed at meals the traditional *Grace before Meals*. But we followed it with a moment of quiet and anyone in the family could add a spontaneous prayer, such as, to ask for healing for a sick friend or relative, or for God's help with a challenge such as a calming of anxiety while taking an important difficult test or to thank God for a safe trip for mom or dad away who had been away on business. Spontaneous prayer does not have to be long, elaborate or personally intimate or revealing. In fact it is learned easily when a person has the opportunity to speak short prayers from the heart on a regular basis. Learning to pray this way, out loud with others, often encourages a person to pray spontaneously, privately and silently, in more in-depth and in more personal ways.

Rote Prayer

Rote Prayer is memorized or recited prayer such as *The Our Father* or *The Hail Mary.* The best time to memorize prayers such as these is in childhood. The easiest ways to teach your children to pray these prayers is to invite them to pray with you at regular times that coincide with your daily activities; meals, bedtime, morning, driving in the car. The earlier you start praying together the easier this will be but don't ever think it is too late! These simple practices can become part of your family's spiritual legacy.

Prayers for a Family to Share

Our Father

Our Father,
Who art in heaven,
hallowed be Thy name;
Thy kingdom come;
Thy will be done on earth as it is in heaven.
Give us this day our daily bread;
and forgive us our trespasses
as we forgive those who trespass against us;
and lead us not into temptation,
but deliver us from evil. Amen.

Hail Mary

Hail Mary, full of grace. The Lord is with thee.
Blessed art thou amongst women,
and blessed is the fruit of thy womb, Jesus.
Holy Mary, Mother of God,
pray for us sinners,
now and at the hour of our death. Amen.

Glory Be

Glory be to the Father,
and to the Son,
and to the Holy Spirit,
as it was in the beginning,
is now, and ever shall be,
world without end. Amen.

Hail Holy Queen

Hail, Holy Queen, Mother of mercy,
our life, our sweetness and our hope.
To thee do we cry, poor banished children of Eve:
to thee do we send up our sighs,
mourning and weeping in this valley of tears.
Turn then, most gracious Advocate,
thine eyes of mercy toward us,
and after this our exile,
show unto us the blessed fruit of thy womb, Jesus.
O clement, O loving, O sweet Virgin Mary! Amen.

Anima Christi

Soul of Christ, make me holy
Body of Christ, be my salvation
Blood of Christ, let me drink your wine
Water flowing from the side of Christ, wash me clean
Passion of Christ, strengthen me
Kind Jesus, hear my prayer
Hide me within your wounds
And keep me close to you
Defend me from the evil enemy
And call me at the hour of my death
To the fellowship of your saints
That I might sing your praise with them
for all eternity. Amen.

Act of Contrition

My God, I am sorry for my sins with all my heart. In choosing to do wrong and failing to do good, I have sinned against you whom I should love above all things. I firmly intend, with your help, to do penance, to sin no more, and to avoid whatever leads me to sin. Our Savior Jesus Christ suffered and died for us. In His name, my God, have mercy. Amen.

Memorare

Remember, O most gracious Virgin Mary,
that never was it known
that anyone who fled to thy protection,
implored thy help
or sought thy intercession,
was left unaided.
Inspired by this confidence,
We fly unto thee, O Virgin of virgins my Mother;
to thee do we come, before thee we stand, sinful and sorrowful;
O Mother of the Word Incarnate,
despise not our petitions,
but in thy mercy hear and answer them. Amen.

Guardian Angel Prayer

Angel of God, my Guardian dear, to whom God's love commits me here, ever this day (or night) be at my side, to light and guard, to rule and guide. Amen.

Grace before Meals

Bless us, O Lord, and these Thy gifts, which we are about to receive from Thy bounty, through Christ our Lord. Amen.

Grace after Meals

We give Thee thanks for all Thy benefits, O Almighty God, who livest and reignest world without end. Amen. May the souls of the faithful departed, through the mercy of God, rest in peace. Amen.

Anyway: The Paradoxical Commandments

People are often unreasonable, illogical and self-centered;
Forgive them anyway.

If you are kind, people may accuse you of selfish, ulterior motives;
Be kind anyway.

If you are successful, you will win some false friends and some true enemies;
Succeed anyway.

If you are honest and frank, people may cheat you;
Be honest and frank anyway.

What you spend years building, someone could destroy overnight;
Build anyway.

If you find serenity and happiness, they may be jealous;
Be happy anyway.

The good you do today, people will often forget tomorrow;
Do good anyway.

Give the world the best you have, and it may never be enough;
Give the world the best you've got anyway.

You see, in the final analysis, it is between you and God;
It was never between you and them anyway!

(Kent M. Keith, 1968)
(Often associated with Mother Teresa's spirituality)

The Prayer of Saint Francis

Lord, make me an instrument of your peace.
Where there is hatred, let me sow love;
Where there is injury, pardon;
Where there is doubt, faith;
Where there is despair, hope;
Where there is darkness, light;
Where there is sadness, joy.

O Divine Master, grant that I may not so much seek
To be consoled as to console;
To be understood as to understand;
To be loved as to love;
For it is in giving that we receive;
It is in pardoning that we are pardoned;
It is in dying that we are born to eternal life.
Amen.

The Serenity Prayer

God grant me the serenity
to accept the things I cannot change;
courage to change the things I can;
and wisdom to know the difference.

Living one day at a time;
Enjoying one moment at a time;
Accepting hardships as the pathway to peace;
Taking, as He did, this sinful world as it is,
not as I would have it;
Trusting that He will make all things right
if I surrender to His Will;
That I may be reasonably happy in this life and supremely
happy with Him Forever in the next.
Amen.

Prayer to the Holy Spirit

Breathe into me Holy Spirit, that all my thoughts may be holy.
Move in me, Holy Spirit, that my work, too, may be holy.
Attract my heart, Holy Spirit, that I may love only what is holy.
Strengthen me, Holy Spirit, that I may defend all that is holy.
Protect me, Holy Spirit, that I always may be holy. Amen.

Come, Holy Spirit

Come, O Holy Spirit, fill the hearts of your faithful and enkindle in them the fire of your love. Send forth your Spirit, and they shall be created. And you shall renew the face of the earth. Amen.

Parents blessing over your children:

Dear God, please bless my child, (Name), today. Protect him/ her in all ways this day. Give him/ her eyes to see ways to love others and show kindness in all of his/ her actions and words. Send your Mother Mary and all the angels to watch over him/her. Amen.

Family Prayer

Work together as a family to develop a prayer that captures your gratitude, intentions, wishes and concerns. Develop a prayer that your family can truly relate to and will you will appreciate saying regularly.

Spontaneous Prayers for a Family to Create

Use the following ideas to pray together as a family using your own words. Pick a different topic at bedtime or for mealtime or before you leave home in the morning for your prayer.

Thank you, God, for…

I saw you, my God, today in…

Dear God, please protect…

Dear God, I am worried about… Please hold my worries and give me peace.

God, help me to do my best in these ways in my life…

Jesus, my savior and brother, walk with me today as I…

We ask you, God to heal…

Jesus, teach us to show care and kindness as you did in your life. Help us to make the world better today by…

"Faith Chest" Spiritual Reflection for Parents

Think about some of the important values you hope to cultivate and pass on to your children.

Reflect on them and write down what those three values are that you want your child(ren) to have and to live.

Write a letter to your child(ren) to express why they are important. Save the letter and give it to him or her sometime when you feel they are old enough to appreciate it.

Chapter Three

FIVE SPIRITUAL HUNGERS

Trust in the LORD with all your heart
and lean not on your own understanding;
in all your ways acknowledge him,
and he will direct your paths.
Proverbs 3, 5-6

Five Spiritual Hungers

Hunger often takes the form of a yearning for something. With physical hunger, our body is longing for physical nourishment. Biological signals alert us to messages from our brain to sustain our bodies with nourishment. Emotionally, we may be aware of hunger for companionship and social relationships that nourish us with conversation, positive feelings and prevent us from experiencing uncomfortable feelings of isolation. Nourishing our emotional life can lead to a greater feeling of satisfaction in our well-being in general. In fact, studies show people live longer and are physically healthier in context of a life rich in social relationships. If you have ever experienced transient or significant depression you may have known the darkness broken by some emotional lifeline of another's companionship or even the compassionate concern expressed from another human being. We live healthier when we are adequately nourished physically and emotionally. Hunger is something we have to pay attention to and attend to or we will not continue to live. Responding to hunger is a most basic instinct. We respond by eating food to the signals of our physical hunger. We respond to our emotional hungers by developing relationships with others and through the human connections in those relationships.

Physical nourishment means more than just taking in a certain amount of calories. The food we eat can be full or empty of nutrients depending on the choices we make in our diet. Have you ever regretted the extra serving of food you didn't need but just impulsively took only to regret how you felt physically afterwards? Or have you ever filled your hunger with a bagful of snack food, only to feel short-term satisfaction but hungry an hour later?

I once was doing mission work in an impoverished rural area and remember being struck with the inventory in the one local convenience store. I realized as I looked around that the store was filled with snack food, processed food, sugar drinks and candy. There was only one small rack of fresh fruits and vegetables available for the local people to choose from of healthy food. The hunger of the people in the community was filled by the food available but it didn't necessarily nourish their bodies. We can feel hunger that we fill in many ways, some with short term satisfactions and some in more lasting ways. Most every one of us has personal experience with the struggle in life to make healthy choices in our diets.

Emotional hunger can be satisfied to different extents by casual conversation and the warmth of friendships. However, we also need deeper connections where we meet another and allow our vulnerabilities, hopes, and dreams to be revealed openly. I sometimes describe this as the relationships where we can be "unedited". We are relating on some core level and these close relationships nourish us emotionally in significant ways. Our social needs are met in many ways by these friendships and deeper relationships. Our emotional health can somewhat be measured by the quality of the relationships that create the social web of our life.

Aside from signals of hunger that may be distorted for psychological reasons most people can tell when they need to eat. Emotionally perceptive people can identify emotional longings they are feeling. However, we as human beings, also experience spiritual hungers that may not be so easily identified or understood. Spiritual longings are a signal from our soul inviting us to live life more deeply and are a gift to "see" the meaning in the life right in front of us. Sometimes that requires us to live with a more practiced sense of gratitude and sometimes it requires us to mine the meaning of the difficulties and challenges we experience in life. Spiritual hunger, the topic of this facet of "The Journey", may be more difficult to distinguish. However it is as real as our physical hunger and as important to be aware of as our hunger for emotional well-being. It is also easy to ignore and to put off attending to… until we have "more time" to devote to it.

Spiritual hunger may be experienced as something less easy to identify than our need for friends or for lunch. It is sometimes described in spiritual literature as emptiness or a longing. Often we can't even identify what *this* is. We can become aware of it in thoughts and feelings that occur intermittently. Think of the teen expressing the comment of adolescent dismissal, "…Whatever", expressing a vague distress that reveals a frustration.

Spiritual hungers can sometimes be revealed to us when we feel our days are just multiple runs around the treadmill. Or spiritual hunger may feel like an acute immediate need, such as the demanding heart that seeks an explanation at the loss from being betrayed or when a loved one has died. Many spiritual writers describe spiritual hunger as an energy that drives us to reflect, to question, to search, to change and, if we are fortunate, to love. It is what some would call a "blessing in disguise" because it often precedes growth and can usher in a deeper experience of life.

We might recognize it in the sentiment in the old song crooned by Rosemary Clooney when she asked, "Is that all there is?" At times haven't most of us asked this question? That question is at the root of our spiritual hunger. We can work so hard at just "doing life" that we can miss the "being in life" that anchors us, gives us stability, perspective, and in many ways holds us together. A good place to find a focus and a sense of perspective is to recognize there is something or someone bigger than ourselves and many of us call that something, faith, and call that someone, God. For purposes of this discussion I will call that being, God, though I know that word can have many different meanings for people. Though this discussion is from a Christian perspective, I know many people around the earth have a different language and perception of the Divine. They are to be respected and appreciated for no one has total understanding of the Divine. I have always found it worthwhile to listen to others describe their experience of who God is. I have learned something from everyone I have taken the time to really listen to who shares their perception of his or her image of God.

It is important, in order to have a spiritual life, to look for some way to relate to God through a faith tradition, spiritual practices, symbols and/or ritual such as prayer or meditation. It is not so important to "get this right", for any relationship is fluid by nature and there are many paths to experience the Divine presence. And who is to judge a personal relationship with God that we each perceive so privately and personally? It is such a gift in life to develop a relationship with God.

A perspective that is challenging but very useful is to have profound appreciation of "my" individuality and worth but also hold within that perspective a paradoxical truth that "I" am also only one part of the community of humanity. We all are created by the same

God. I am a unique child of God. I have intrinsic value, as do all of God's children.

It is difficult to nourish ourselves spiritually if we do not recognize some things we long for are spiritual in nature, and nourishing our soul may be life enhancing and life changing. Coming to awareness that what we really need to address, our restlessness and search for meaning, is spiritual, and attending to our spiritual needs is worthy of our time and energy. It is often where we must all begin and begin, again and again, in our journey of life. Most of us are easily distracted from the inner life by the world around us. We tend to fill our spiritual hungers with physical things, like food, or emotional short term distractions like entertainment.

While anything spiritual is difficult to depict in words and the images we use to try to speak of God will always fall so short of adequate, we must try to give faith a language in order to share what we have experienced and to teach and to learn from each other. And so we can ask, "What are spiritual hungers"? How might we describe them? What form do they take on our human journey?

Here are five I have come to identify in listening to thousands of people describe their spiritual quest:

- Hunger for Meaning
- Hunger for Intimacy
- Hunger for Belonging
- Hunger for Love
- Hunger for Inner Peace

THE HUNGER FOR MEANING

The Hunger for Meaning

We all have a need to find *meaning* in life. Each of us has a need to discover *purpose* in life. This might be framed as having an internal motivation to know that who we are matters. We each have a drive to have a life that counts. Making the priority to become the person God longs for us to be is to how we find that meaning. It is to understand material success, good health, and achievement, are gifts we may be given but the character we develop, the values we cultivate, the way in which we love God and others is what ultimately counts spiritually. Learning to use the gifts we are given for loving intentions is true success. Doing the best we can and finding our purpose with the life we are given is the mark of someone on the spiritual path. It is not so much what our life looks like as judged by others but how it would be judged by God's yardstick of love that matters.

This hunger to know the meaning of our lives is the subject of poetry, art and literature. It was most poignantly described by Viktor Frankl in his book, "Man's Search for Meaning". Between 1942 and 1945, Frankl spent time in four different Nazi concentration camps. He experienced his own suffering, the loss of his family and was witness to perhaps the greatest atrocities systematically applied from human beings to other human beings in the atrocities of the holocaust. Out of these experiences and his desire to live life following these years, Frankl asked and responded to the most perplexing questions humans ask: Why is there suffering? How can such cruelty and evil exist in the world? What matters in life? How does one move on from the painful aspects and difficult experiences of life? What matters when you have lost much? How does one incorporate any kind of significant suffering and trauma into a meaningful life? And how do we live with optimism when we realize there is always the potential for suffering and often it is randomly assigned?

These really only begin the questions related to the hunger for meaning. For even a life where one has not experienced significant suffering can lack perceived meaning if we don't have a lens to see beauty, hope, faith or love. Perhaps the greatest sin of modern times is taking for granted the good that is ours in life. To wake every morning and appreciate the promise of a new day is a spiritual insight. To be able to live and to find joy in the moment is a spiritual gift. To be able to see the connectedness of all of life and God's love for everyone is at the heart of the spiritual quest.

For Frankl, the response to having experienced the trials he did set him on an intense journey to satisfy a deep, deep hunger for meaning. Frankel writes:

> The way in which a man accepts his fate and all the suffering it entails, the way in which he takes up his cross, gives him ample opportunity — even under the most difficult circumstances — to add a deeper meaning to his life. He may remain brave, dignified and unselfish. Or in the bitter fight for self-preservation he may forget his human dignity and become no more than an animal.
> (Victor Frankl, Man's search for Meaning)

The spiritual hunger for meaning actually begins to be addressed, first, by identifying the deepest questions we have as human beings. These are the, "why" questions. They are *spiritual questions,* and we need to recognize they will never be satisfied by logic or reason. To honor them requires an ability to utilize a different kind of thinking.

One way to image this kind of thinking, is that it is contemplative. That term expresses a thought process that invites us reflect on our life by simply observing it and not judging it. It is to acquire the ability "to think" about the experiences of our life as just that, "our experiences". The good and bad, the sweet and painful, the mundane and soulful, are what make up the fabric of our own personal story. To grow spiritually we have to learn to consider ourselves as blessed and broken in a non-judgmental way. To live in a sincere search for meaning, in whatever life circumstances we find ourselves in, is a spiritual practice. It requires cultivating a reflective intelligence, which is an ability to strengthen our thinking capacity, to reflect, to not react too quickly, but to allow the meaning of life to reveal itself in time. This is most often achieved by learning to "live in the moment" and regularly reflect on the moments that make up our lives. Some people call this practicing "mindfulness".

One aspect of this practice is to consider employing it in our relationships. We can practice this reflection and contemplation when we are engaged in conversation with another. We can learn to just listen to another share the perspective they see of life from their point of view. Even if we totally disagree with another there is value in simply listening, deeply and "learning" from them the perspective of what they "see" and "feel". To be heard in a respectful way is a great gift in life.

Another key to cultivating our spiritual life is to engage this not only with others but also with ourselves. Some people find it easier to "understand" and "accept" others than themselves. But to love others we must also learn to do this with ourselves.

Consider, however hard you have been on yourself that you are a child of God and in many ways you have done the best you can with you have been given. Allow for a few minutes each day just to reflect on the day and invite God into your contemplative time. Invite God simply to be present to you as you consider your truth. This practice can be healing and enlightening. If there is anxiety, depression or discomfort in this time of contemplation, ask God to heal whatever is the source of that feeling. Call the Divine Healer into your mind, heart and soul. Ask God to be with you, like a child would ask a parent to lie with them before sleep comes to them when in bed at night.

A key understanding that will guide you on this path to find meaning in your life journey is to consciously live embracing life within the notion of "paradox". Accepting the paradox of life means that we can and, in fact have to, hold both love and loss in figurative *open hands*, not grasping or demanding anything but simply accepting this is what life is. No matter how much we wish many things in life were logical or fair or just or went our way, or we distort reality to live with that illusion, many important things in life are ambiguous, unclear and never will be uncomplicated. In fact, the parts of life we might have found most painful or unacceptable, when acknowledged and held in contemplative thought, or healed by time, love, or forgiveness may become our greatest blessings. Have you ever heard the phrase we become strong when we heal in the broken places? As humans some of these experiences take time to heal and the irony is that we cannot force healing but we can learn to trust that what hurts us will heal in time and that process is nurtured by tenderness, mercy and ultimately living with hope. This is true for us and for others.

Mother Teresa said, "God writes straight with crooked lines." This describes what she saw from a life reflected upon on a regular basis. You may discover this is true for yourself if you engage in reflective practices over time. It requires an ability to see what is seen when one is able to "look back" over time and not seek judgment but understanding of life. You may find it is an extraordinary gift to give yourself and others to discover a capacity in you for forgiveness.

To find meaning in life is a personal quest. No one can "give" it to you but you can choose it over and over again in your life. When we have done this often enough we will find some peace and deeper value in the "now" and in "what was." We will know a satiating of our spiritual hunger as we learn to find meaning in the everyday as well as in the difficulties and losses.

Reflection, as well as, the regular practice of gratitude will help us to do that. The conscious practice of forgiveness and reminding ourselves we are a unique child of God in the good company of all of God's children will lead us to the nourishment our soul is longing to know.

We will find our meaning and purpose in life as we come to value what God values and learn to love what God loves. And God loves me and you and all of our brothers and sisters on this earth.

Exercise: The Hunger for Meaning

For where your treasure is, there your heart will also be.
(Matthew 6:21)

Meaning in life can be elusive. Whether or not we find meaning in life can be critical. A sense of meaning can be subtle and we can miss it if we don't pay attention. The sense that what we spend our life doing is of value or has purpose, such as the long term and intangible role of raising children or caring for an elderly loved one can be disregarded as "what we do" and we may miss that in that act of caring a loving and generous person is "who we become". What gives life meaning is often connected to what we hold as our deepest and truest values. Knowing what we truly value can help us to identify what does or can bring meaning to us. Sometimes just living faithfully our values can create meaning in life.

What would you identify as the greatest purpose in your life?

Value Clarification Exercise

While our values may not be something we recognize as spiritual they may be what distinguish us soulfully as a human being. Sit in a quiet place and focus on your breathing. Allow yourself a few moments of peaceful contemplation. Try not to be distracted by wandering thoughts. Simply acknowledge them and refocus on your breathing.

When you have remained quiet in your body and mind for a few minutes respond to the following questions in writing, personal reflection or in dialogue with another.

1. Who is someone you have admired and feel you are a better person for having spent time with this person?

2. Name two or three qualities you have admired in others as you reflect on your relationships.

3. What is an experience you had that you treasure?

4. What is one thing you believe is worth "living for"?

5. What are three values you hold? Describe them in a word or phrase.

Sit quietly and simply allow your mind to find an image or word that embodies one of those values.

Reflective Intelligence Exercise

We develop our reflective intelligence by practicing "reflection". This can be a challenge to the western mind because it can feel passive and the opposite of "accomplishing something" and can even be considered "non-productive." It is anything but that! To learn to think reflectively is one of the highest functions a human being can achieve. Many of the great spiritual leaders in history came to new insights about humanity through reflective thinking. Consider Gandhi's insight of change through non-violence.

To achieve a developed reflective intelligence requires cultivating the ability to observe and to contemplate life and not to judge experiences as simply good or bad but as the layered complex realities many of them are and also to appreciate the simplicity and beauty in the ordinary.

Sit quietly alone for a few minutes and consider the following:

1. Think about someone you admire. Decide the next time you are with that person you will listen to him or her with great care. Write your intention down to remember to do this in your next encounter with the person.

2. Think of someone you don't understand or with whom you disagree about something. Decide the next time you are with that person you will listen to him or her with great care. Write your intention down to remember to do this in your next encounter with the person.

3. Think of a significant experience you had in the past and sit quietly and reflect upon it. Try not to judge your feelings, just observe them. Ask God to come into your reflection and heal any hurt, pain, regret or discomfort around this experience.

THE HUNGER FOR INTIMACY

The Hunger for Intimacy

God comes to you disguised in your life.
(Paula D'Arcy)

The spiritual hunger for intimacy is the desire we have as human beings to "be known." We all want someone; some other person to "know" who we are and, here is the important part, to love us as we are. Some spiritual writers call *being known* in this way, being in touch with the "true self". This is the person we are under our roles, titles, and illusions. It is how God sees us, as unconditionally valuable and loveable. For some of us it takes some work to get to this point to find that loveable core, that true self, the person we are if someone could understand all that has gone into making us who we are, all that has motivated us, wounded us, the hidden parts or the parts we may believe are hidden. (Though we may not realize it, often the parts aren't really that "hidden"!)

An irony of this is that we most often find this for ourselves and fill this spiritual hunger in giving this kind of regard and care to another. As we choose to relate spiritually with another, personally, we may find in some way of cosmic justice this gift comes back to us. It may not, in fact, come from the same person we have extended that understanding to but perhaps it comes to us from some other person, somewhere, at a different time.

You may ask, "Does this mean I don't hold another accountable or expect certain behaviors from them?" It does not mean that. In a setting such as work or even in a family or community we can hold certain expectations for and from others. I can and should expect another to treat me with respect and kindness, to do what they say they are going to do, to keep their word, to represent the values you have mutually agreed to live by. And we can and should extend these same expectations of others.

What I am describing is more an inner practice of consciously living in such a way as to choose to live, as the Prayer of St. Francis reminds us, in peaceful and compassionate ways:

Lord, make me an instrument of your peace.
Where there is hatred, let me sow love;
where there is injury, pardon;
where there is doubt, faith;
where there is despair, hope;
where there is darkness, light;
and where there is sadness, joy.

O Divine Master, grant that I may not so much seek
to be consoled as to console;
to be understood as to understand;
to be loved as to love.
For it is in giving that we receive;
it is in pardoning that we are pardoned;
and it is in dying that we are born to eternal life. Amen

The prayer calls us not so much to a recipe for life as a perspective to embrace in our relationships. It is an invitation to live in a way that seeks and offers intimacy in life. I once read the story of a woman who lost a loved one in a tragic accident when she was a young woman. Her work later in life was as a counselor and she found herself counseling a woman who had killed another person in an incident that involved a similar accident. She acknowledged it took some time and prayer on her part to sustain the relationship. But she ultimately realized, through the relationship and by extending this woman her respectful listening, she came to see the other side of the pain that she had experienced. She could have chosen a different path and it would have been reasonable for her to decline this opportunity. But the healing she found, not through a deliberate effort on her own behalf, but by simply being willing to "know" this other person, no doubt was beneficial for both of them.

This is the kind of intimacy that is at the core of filling the spiritual hunger. It is being willing to connect with another person in such a way that it actually connects us with God. It allows us to experience closeness with another that is real and deep. So often we are willing to put ourselves out, expend energy on superficial relationships, "cocktail party" relationships. I think of them as filling the moment with conversation that only skims the surface of the gifts we have for each other. What if we each focused on treating each other in such a manner that paves the way to see another as God sees that person and to love another as God loves him or her? What would life be like for us and for them if we did that?

What this spiritual hunger is "yearning for" may require what is most challenging for us to give. That is to extend compassion and care to ourselves. We must first and consistently practice this with ourselves. I must decide the only way to live authentically is to be on the path of discovering that "true self" and loving who I find myself to really be, not some idealized version of who I am or a façade of who I wish I was. This kind of living requires I speak from my heart, tell the truth in kindness to myself and others; to determine that the gift of my life is so important I have no choice but to live as if I value and treasure each moment given to me. If this is my quest, then how I use my time, spend my money, speak to others, fill my mind with words and images will become the expression of my spirituality.

The other side of intimacy requires I not only give these gifts to others on a continual basis but that I am willing to reveal that "true self" to others. It would not be prudent to think that these kinds of sacred relationships of trust are extended to every person, without thought and trust that this gift is understood and received with the same respect it is given. This is not to indicate we need to "tell everyone everything about ourselves." Our desire for authenticity, to discover and be our "true self" that we strive for consistently, does not mean that we don't maintain privacy about certain things. That is always a right and, in fact, a responsibility of self-care, to have the discretion to determine what the level of self-disclosure and vulnerability we determine is good for ourselves and to whom we extend this depth of friendship.

In these decisions, Jesus Christ is an outstanding model of someone who lived consistently as his "true self" but also made thoughtful choices about revealing himself to others. At the Jordan River, he humbly welcomed John the Baptist to inaugurate his public ministry with his Baptism. (Luke 3: 23) He did not, however, explain his identity at that time.

When he asked the disciples, "Who do people say that I am?" wasn't he gauging what to reveal about himself and didn't he then reserve the right to ascertain when and how to reveal himself. "Now is not the time I wish to share with everyone who I am and what my mission is." (Matt 8: 27-30) Jesus modeled for us willingness to live an authentic life while reserving the right to determine what to share with another. In the end, Jesus was true to himself with everyone, his friends and his enemies. He did this over time and he determined when and what to reveal in his relationships while retaining an authenticity of his own personhood. He also found a way to have friendships so deep and true, he changed his disciples' lives so profoundly, that it is still affecting us today.

Why is the longing for intimacy a spiritual hunger? Because ultimately we all long to feel accepted in the presence of another and ultimately *know* in the most vulnerable places in our heart and soul that we are accepted by God. We long not to travel through life alone.

In Scripture the phrase, "Be not afraid," is repeated hundreds of times. The gift of true intimacy brings the trust that allows us to live without fear. These kinds of relationships of intimacy that weave into our lives are the antidote to fear. We are unlikely to live at that level of trust without the confidence and security that loving relationships provide. There is no shorter path to self-acceptance than a life paved rich with people who know, accept and love us, friends and family, who surround and ground us.

Exercise: The Hunger for Intimacy

Finally, brothers, whatever is true, whatever is honorable, whatever is just, whatever is pure, whatever is lovely, whatever is gracious, if there is any excellence and if there is anything worthy of praise, think about these things.

Keep on doing what you have learned and received and heard and seen in me. Then the God of peace will be with you.

(Philippians4:8-9)

Spend some time reading this Scripture over several times.

Consider what you find:

Honorable

Just

Lovely

Gracious

Of excellence

Worthy of praise

Make note of these things and try to remember to focus on them in life rather than your disappointments and frustrations.

Seeing Through God's Eyes Exercise

We all want someone, at least one other person to know us and to love us. This kind of relationship that we most often find within a family or a friendship is a sacred gift. This person can reflect back to us who we are. In this relationship we can appreciate another person in the totality of their being, in their beauty and their vulnerability. Such a union is not always easy to find in life but if found is never lost, not even in death.

One key to finding this in life is to learn to see yourself as you truly are, as God sees you, loveable, understandable, forgiven, and treasured.

After taking a short time in stillness respond to these questions as truthfully as you can. Invite God into your thoughts and reflections. You can use these questions for prayerful reflection, journaling or dialogue with another person you trust.

1. You are a delightful person. What is one thing that makes you delightful?

2. Few of us get through life without wounds and scars. The important thing is to own them and allow whatever process is necessary to heal. What is a wound or scar you know you have? In your mind, tenderly be with it. Hold the memory without judgment of yourself or anyone else, simply allow yourself to remember it.

3. Think of one person who loved you as a child. Contemplate as much about that person as you can. In your mind, allow that person to look at you, hold you, or touch you. As you bring this meditation to an end in your heart thank that person for loving you.

Who am I? Exercise

Take about 20 to 30 minutes of time alone for self-reflection and, within the page below, using words, pictures or symbols, share a vision of *who you are,* physically, emotionally, intellectually and spiritually. Focus on discovering, uncovering and identifying who you become when you own "all of you". You have a beauty that evolves from your experiences and years. In the gifts and challenges of your individual journey, from the "wheat and weeds" of your experiences, your life forms layers into a kind of richness of who you are. This is who God created and continues to know and love.

THE HUNGER FOR BELONGING

The Hunger for Belonging

No, in all these things we are more than conquerors through him who loved us. For I am sure that neither death nor life, nor angels nor rulers, nor things present nor things to come, nor powers, nor height nor depth, nor anything else in all creation, will be able to separate us from the love of God in Christ Jesus our Lord.

(Romans 8:37-39)

Related to the spiritual hunger of real intimacy is the longing to have a sense of belonging in life. A sense of belonging comes from "getting" that we are part of something bigger than ourselves. The Franciscan priest, Fr. Richard Rohr, has done much work in the area of spirituality. He talks about our spiritual development in the first half of life and the second half of life. Fr. Rohr believes that what we do in the first half of life prepares us for the second half of life to have a spiritual perspective to negotiate all the gifts and challenges that life might bring us. He says that in the first half of life we build a "container" that will carry us through what life brings us in the second half of life. The gift of a spiritual formation is that it helps us to understand that something bigger than ourselves holds us, carries us. He images this, as the container that we need to develop that metaphorically surrounds us. We can image this as an outer container that holds us but really is the reality of God that holds us. We are not the creators of ourselves, those we love, nor did we create the world. The sense of belonging comes from knowing we are a part of something bigger than ourselves. And that Divine being is holding and protecting us.

My friend had a very well-known spiritual director we will call Dolores. Since she was an eminent person, I was curious as to what wisdom she had shared with my friend. When she would come back from seeing her I would always ask, "So what did Dolores say?" My friend always replied, Dolores said, "God is bigger." I loved that answer and have thought about it countless times though the years. It is so succinct, wise and true.

My friend was in her early thirties. She grew up in what she calls "The God loves you, draw a picture era." She and many of her generation were trying to develop enough "experienced faith" to believe in a sense of belonging. Father Richard Rohr might say they are trying to build a container to carry them into the maturing of their lives and the spiritual resources they might need.

If you have not done that, built that solid vessel, to carry you spiritually through life, you may want to give that thought and attention. If you are a parent you have the opportunity to help your child build a strong container to carry him or her through life. I have always said I wish and hope my children and all those I love have enough faith to hold onto when they need it. I want them to have a faith to secure and anchor them after I am gone, when I cannot be there for them. To me that is the core of what faith in God does for us. It is to know we are held and loved by something more than we can understand with our mind but can know in our heart. It is to know that we belong to God.

The context that gives us that feeling of belonging to "something bigger" is built when faith is experienced, through prayer, ritual and relationships. Enough experiences need to occur to create something that is strong enough to hold us through the journey of life, the betrayals we may experience, the challenges we surely will experience, the losses we all will eventually experience. It is the strength of the spiritual life we have developed that holds us, that we push against, in times of doubt and struggle in life, and that we stretch when we need to create an understanding of life to hold us in the bad times as well as the good times. But without the foundation of the spiritual foundation being strong enough, what can hold us as we toss and turn on the journey of life?

This spiritual footing is where we learn to trust, really trust, so as to stake our lives on it. It is the security we come to believe in, beyond our own strength and resources. It is to believe not just in ourselves, but also in others and ultimately in God. It is actions, and words that are repeated and repeated, until they become part of the fabric of beliefs and values woven into our lives. The tightness of the weave, the security the vessel provides and engenders in us, is determined by the priority we give it in life. It gives us a sense of belonging and helps us know we are spiritually anchored through life.

To know a sense of belonging often comes not in one large or complete act but in many, many, smaller experiences and through experiences in communities where we have a sense of welcome, familiarity and acceptance. If you don't have such a faith community, keep looking. We are not meant to go it alone spiritually.

Find a group that serves others. Help out with a meal program or some mission of outreach. Find a prayer group that prays in a way that is comfortable for you. Find a ministry in your church that speaks to you and serve in it. Find a volunteer opportunity somewhere that is out of your comfort zone and try it with an open heart. Watch for someone who is more lonely than you are and just try to smile and talk to them. We need to have concrete experiences as well as faith to have a sense that we are not alone. We each need to know we belong to something bigger and someone bigger who guides and protects us. Seek a spiritual guide, director or companion to help you find where and how you belong.

I have framed this discussion of addressing this spiritual hunger in a response of a religious tradition. That is because that is how I have witnessed people over time grow. My belief is that we are well-nourished and nurtured by a religious tradition. This is not to judge those who do not choose to be part of a faith community. It is just my observation that life shared in some sense of a caring community of faithful others enriches and anchors individuals.

It seems the spiritual wisdom of a faith tradition that might be hundreds or thousands of years old and has guided and supported others through all of that time would have more insight and wisdom than I could discover alone in just my lifetime.

And that is why, as imperfect as a community can be (including my presence in it!) I choose to travel with others who also are trying to negotiate life in shared beliefs, values and practices. A religious tradition and a faith community offer morals and values bigger than my own feelings, knowledge or experience from which I draw strength, direction and wisdom. I am not floating out here alone.

I am cared for and protected by the God who created me and loves me and to whom I will be united beyond this life and who is holding my loved ones who have died. I am held by the God who created me, loves me and to whom I belong. I am part of “family” united by common beliefs, values, practices and traditions that strengthen me and in fact may hold me together when I may feel I am “falling apart”. These are also the people and the God who surrounds me with joy and celebrates the good in life with me. The sharp edges in life are so much easier to negotiate in the context of supportive others. The best in life is so much sweeter shared with others who love us and God who delights in us.

Exercise: The Hunger for Belonging

> *But now, O Israel, the Lord who created you says: "Do not be afraid, for I have ransomed you. I have called you by name; you are mine. When you go through deep waters and great trouble, I will be with you."*
>
> *(Isaiah 43:1-2)*

A sense of belonging is a strong spiritual need we all have and though it takes different forms at different times in our life, the need never really goes away. Review where you have felt this sense of belonging in your life? How have you expanded your world to include others so that they might have a sense of belonging in life?

My Sense of Belonging

Consider the following designated times of your life. Reflect on where or from whom you have developed your sense of belonging at different times of your life. Only respond to the phases that are appropriate for your life.

- In my Childhood I had a sense of belonging from:

- In my Adolescence I had a sense of belonging from:

- In my Early Adulthood I had a sense of belonging from:

- When Raising Children I had a sense of belonging from:

- As an Empty Nester I had a sense of belonging from:

- As a Single Person I had a sense of belonging from:

- As a Widow, Widower, Divorced Person I had a sense of belonging from:

- In my Faith Community I had a sense of belonging from:

- In my Prayer Life I had a sense of belonging from:

- In my Older Years I had a sense of belonging from:

- In the Next Phase of My Life I hope to have a sense of belonging from:

The Container

What formed or is forming the container for the first half of life for you? If you are in the first half of life what might you do to weave a stronger spiritual container for your second half of life?

Above the "container" illustrated below, make notes on what you hope will spiritually "carry you through" the second half of life.

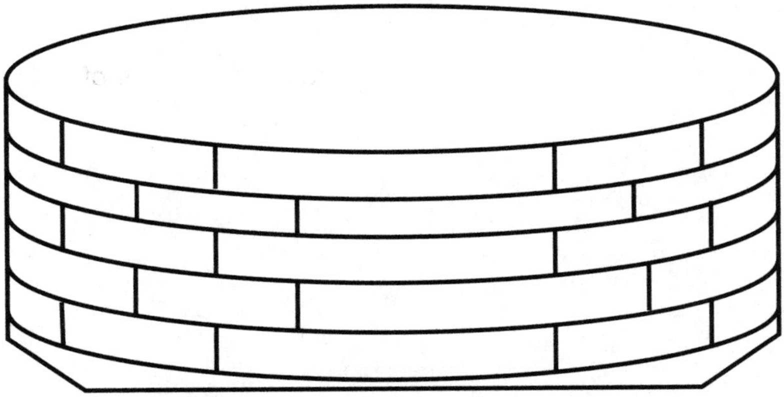

THE HUNGER FOR LOVE

The Hunger for Love

So faith, hope, and love remain, these three,
but the greatest of these is love
(1 Corinthians 13:13)

Of all the spiritual hungers that drive us and create purpose in our lives and is the source of both the joy and heartbreak none is more profound or critical than love. To define love would be a folly on my part. We can describe our experience of it but perhaps Scripture offers the best description of *the spiritual hunger of love* most concisely:

> *Beloved, let us love one another, because love is of God; everyone who loves is begotten by God and knows God. Whoever is without love does not know God, for God is love. In this way the love of God was revealed to us: God sent his only Son into the world so that we might have life through him. In this is love: not that we have loved God, but that he loved us... Beloved, if God so loved us, we must also love one another. No one has ever seen God. Yet, if we love one another, God remains in us, and his love is brought into perfection in us…. God is love, and whoever remains in love remains in God and God in him.*
>
> *(1 John 4: 7-12, 16)*

There are many forms and kinds of love. Romantic love between individuals is a precious gift, as we have explored in the section on couple relationships. While that is a beautiful and precious part of life, that is not the meaning of love I refer to here. The spiritual hunger that is love's source is not in the world and not in another human person. There truly is, at the root of the spiritual journey a longing for the transcendent. There is a desire to find a way to connect, to be nourished and to live in the flow of this transcendent love. It is to know love that is eternal and everlasting. The source of this love is found in God.

Scripture tells us it is not us who "loves first" but God who first loves us. Many of us struggle with that belief that we are at our deepest core, loveable. Often we are so very aware of our limitations, failures and mistakes. Sometimes we can even define ourselves by them rather than by our innate goodness. When we look through the lens of our own limited understanding we can so often come up short. The stress and pace of our current times can exacerbate that sense that we aren't good enough, not keeping up, not meeting even our own, sometimes unrealistic, expectations. This inner dialogue can cause us to actually feel un-loveable.

To understand the love we are hungering for spiritually, we need to "borrow" the lens of God who sees us, as he saw the "woman at the well", perhaps as wounded, hurt, misguided, but precious and loveable.

I once worked and studied with a psychologist who was a deeply spiritual person. In an attempt to help people understand themselves and others he spoke about what I will call "the God view" of us. He said that if you could lay out every thought, interaction, influence, of each moment and of every relationship of a person's life, their choices and behaviors would make perfect sense. This, he said is the way God knows us. There is nothing that can't be understood, forgiven, appreciated or loved about us by God. God is the source of such love. Often we hunger to be loved in such a way. We long to be known and accepted, not for some aspect or a dimension of the person we are that the world perceives. We long to be known as the whole person we are if we were known, understood and accepted completely and unconditionally. We long for love from someone who can love us in such a way.

As we come to be able to live knowing we are loved like this we begin to have the ability to love others in this way. Scripture invites us to love one another in this way. "Beloved, if God so loved us, we must also love one another." (1 John 4:11) Sometimes we have to work hard at this. I know when I find someone difficult to love or maybe even "to like" I may need to ask God to help me see with that God-lens of love. It takes a great deal of compassion and care to value this kind of love and practice it on a daily basis. The practice and commitment to love others consistently in life is our intention to address the hunger for love. It can also be a relief to know it isn't our job to have to judge others. We simply are asked to extend to others the care we would wish for ourselves.

Sometimes we get a glimpse of this in this life, not often, but if we are blessed we may have moments for such insight. For me becoming a grandparent has been such an experience. I was in the waiting room with other family members, holding vigil as my daughter-in-law, Lisa, and my son, Jon, were in the delivery room through a long and difficult labor with their first child, my first grandchild. After what seemed like such a long wait, Jon came to the waiting room door, and motioned for us to come in. Through the threshold I could see this tiny bundle of a person, eyes swollen shut from her hard journey into the world. Jon said, "I want you to meet Maria Katharine." I looked at her in utter amazement. I couldn't speak. I think I squeaked out some sounds and tears of amazing joy. But what ran through my head still makes me smile and puzzles me to this day. In my mind, my heart said, "Maria Katharine… I would die for you… if a train were speeding toward you I would jump in front of it. If there are burning coals I would walk across them to get to you! I would give my life for you." Honestly, that is the strange thought that went through my mind. Surely, this seemed a bit of an unusual thought upon meeting this lovely baby girl. I would have imagined I could have come up with something more grandmotherly, like, "What a beautiful child!"

What I think my heart was saying was. "I love you and you are mine." (Isaiah 43:1) We were not in any danger and Maria did not need saving. It was so weird a thought I didn't speak it out loud but it came to me so clear and true and I believe I would stand behind it in little and critical ways forever. It was as if I knew, at that moment, if not who God is, how God loves. Is that not the spirit of the God who gave his Son that we might live?

I have wondered if when we die we are met with that kind of overwhelming and beautiful love. That is the way I imagine my parents were greeted by God when they left this earth in death. I believe God, with open arms called to them and said something like,

"Carmen, Bill, I love you and you are mine." I hope that God greeted them with the same "over the top" welcome with which my heart greeted Maria.

This kind of love was eloquently expressed by Victor Frankl, and ironically he discovered it in the wisdom he forged from searching for meaning in the horror of the concentration camps:

> *A thought transfixed me: for the first time in my life I saw the truth as it is set into song by so many poets, proclaimed as the final wisdom by so many thinkers. The truth - that love is the ultimate and the highest goal to which man can aspire. Then I glimpsed the meaning of the great secret that human poetry and human thought and belief have to impart: The salvation of man is through love and in love. I understood how a man who has nothing left in this world still knows bliss, be it only for a brief moment, in the contemplation of his beloved.*
>
> *(Viktor Frankl)*

So in the great commandments Jesus summarized "the whole law", "Love God above all things. Love yourself and your neighbor as you would want to be loved." And so we have a map to fill this spiritual hunger for love. To give what we long to have is the paradox of finding it. To leave a legacy of love is the choice of generosity in life but ultimately it is exactly how we come to find what we most need.

Exercise: The Hunger for Love

If you judge people, you have no time to love them.

(Mother Teresa)

Think of someone who has hurt you, who you do not understand or simply don't like. If you have the opportunity, have a conversation with the person. Try to talk with them while you keep an open mind. If that is not possible write a description that would tell them how you imagine God sees them.

Exercise: Love Letter

I have found the paradox, that if you love until it hurts,
there can be no more hurt, only more love.
(Mother Teresa)

Think of someone, living or not living, who has loved you unconditionally. Write them a letter and tell them what you think of them, how they made you feel, what a difference they made in your life.

Dear ______________ ,

Love,

____

THE HUNGER FOR INNER PEACE

The Hunger for Inner Peace

Therefore, as God's chosen people, holy and dearly loved, clothe yourselves with compassion, kindness, humility, gentleness and patience.
(Colossians 3:12)

The only thing more difficult than finding inner peace is to sustain it. Yet it is a foundational hunger we continue to long for throughout life. Children raised in healthy families should have childhoods consisting far more of peace than lack of it. Adulthood with its complexities, challenges and choices can accelerate the need for intentionally cultivating inner peace. What often would feed the hunger for inner peace is what many of us find most difficult to sacrifice: activity and noise. Periods of time in quiet and stillness aren't easy to achieve. Such solitude and stillness can "feel" unproductive.

I write this not because I have achieved a constant or even a consistent state of inner peace but because it is something I both struggle with and value. The fast pace of many of our lives is not necessarily conducive to inner peace. It often is not essentially emotionally or spiritually healthy and yet the treadmill of the very active life is not easy to disembark. And to exacerbate the issue, the world does not reward prayer, meditation or even intentional slowing down, relaxation or rest. So there is little external reward for integrating stillness into our "busyness".

In many ways the more we do, the more we are valued. Is that why the helpless young and the declining old can be valued less by some than the achieving, strong and powerful in our world? While inner peace, I believe, is something we dearly hunger for, it requires some practices we can find challenging, for example, practicing stillness, sitting in some quiet space and listening to and waiting on the Lord.

Waiting and inactivity of any kind is not a beloved quality in our culture. A whole discipline has been created around time management. The ability to multitask is, for many, a source of pride. I know personally I struggle with the issue, because to tell the truth, I often judge the value of my day by *what I get done*, *how much I can accomplish*.

In listening sessions I conducted for a research project I did, I found that often people described the tension they feel between the outward demands on their time and dedicating time to what they really most deeply value and believe important, like family, faith and friendships. This isn't a problem that naturally just eases over time or seems to improve as we get older. Parents with young children or older children express this stress, young adults and retired folks lament the gap between what is important to them and how they spend their most precious gift of time.

I think of the "O" Antiphon prayer, "My soul in stillness waits". How difficult is it to allow your soul to wait in stillness? It seems to me there are two questions we need to ask ourselves. In light of the tension between our busyness and the call to allow our soul to wait in stillness we need to ask: *What am I waiting for* and *how do I wait*?

What are we waiting for? We need to know what we are waiting for. I believe we are waiting to trust that God - God's self - is holding us safe secure and we can be at peace. Can we trust that God has something better for us than we can imagine? The prophets in Scripture propose for us, what the future would be if we trust, not the reality we now see, but the reality that could be if we live in trust with God. The prophet, Isaiah literally names that "God Presence". He says God is, Emmanuel, "God is with us". Perhaps what we wait for, in the quiet and stillness, is that true, deep, knowing that God is with us. In a busy, noisy world, can we be still and wait to know the *Sacred* in the silence?

I believe the second question, "*How do I wait*" is related. The best example of "waiting well" that I ever experienced was the vigil waiting with my family in the last weeks of my Dad's life in hospice care. It was the gracefulness with which my Dad waited that showed me the dignity and beauty of waiting. He was waiting for what I imagined, he most dreaded, to die and leave us, his beloved family. I knew he was scared and sad yet he still maintained a curiosity to wonder in life. Even in this, his waiting time, it was apparent, in the way he related to his family and his caretakers, that he savored every human interaction and appreciated the smallest gesture of kindness shown to him. He relinquished the considerable status, power and resources he had in this life, even his ability to physically care for his own basic needs himself, with the grace that said he knew, it had all been a gift. He waited in a quiet trust. The trust that is known in the heart and in the soul that, we make our plans, we do our best to manage the time given us, but in this life and in any life to come, the greatest treasure, through it all, is that God is with us. God is always with us. Our faithful God *waits* on us… just for the opportunity to be with us…when we have the time…

If finding inner peace is discovered in stillness and waiting, sustaining inner peace is found in continually seeking a "centering" of our life that develops from our willingness to value and practice reflective thinking. We live and interact in the external world but a key to sustaining inner peace is to learn to "center ourselves" in our inner world, not the external world. Of course this means we have to trust the spiritual nature of our humanity and that can be a leap of faith for rational people. Those who have cultivated practices of prayer and/or meditation may understand the concept of "centering" life from their experiences rooted in a reflective perspective achieved in prayer and meditation.

If you have had the privilege of witnessing a birth have you not been amazed by new life emerging from its mother? In the manifestation of life, in flesh and blood, do we not see a spiritual event we often call the miracle of birth? And who has not had some or many experiences of the spiritual connection of a touch, a hug, a glance of a loved one? The paradox is that we will find the spiritual truth in attentiveness to our humanness. Awareness and appreciation of the gifts of being human are simply astounding: laughter, music, physical activity, friendships, learning and loving, just to name a few. And often in attending to nature itself we come most in touch with appreciation of the spiritual values in life.

The more willing we are to engage in practices that help to center ourselves in this inner state of awareness, the more we increase the chances of living like we may have as a child, with more inner peace than lack of it. The key can be to engage in these practices on a more "regular" basis than an occasional and sporadic basis. Like a weekend athlete who overdoes it going out running full force without regular practice leading up to it, the hurried person may find it challenging to engage in regular periods of prayer, meditation, or even reflection of life experiences. But like physical conditioning, these practices can be so beneficial. If you are a person of faith there is even a deeper benefit. It is in the stillness, the waiting, the silence that many spiritual guides advise us the relationship with God is cultivated, deepened, strengthened.

Often inner peace is related to how we live in peace in the outer world. This requires that we know what our own personal priorities are. Make peace with attending to the things that are important to you in your own values and beliefs. Be willing to let go of what isn't really central to what you deem worth your time and energy. Be attentive to the people and purposes that are important to you. The more we can be true to ourselves the more internal peace will flow naturally.

If forgiveness is necessary to ask from another person or to give to someone consider working toward that. Be generous. Often the hurts we carry drains our time and emotional and spiritual energy. Life is so short and burdens of hurt are heavy to carry. Pray for those you can't forgive and ask for the grace to be able to let go of the injury at some point. Trust in God's generous heart to heal what keeps you from living in peace more often than in fear, and anxiety.

Each one of us has to find his or her peace from within. And inner peace is necessary to live in the sweet spot of life. Slow down. Breathe. Rest. Linger the words of the psalmist: "Be still and know that I am God". (Psalm 46:10)

Exercise: The Hunger for Inner Peace

Have patience with everything that remains
unsolved in your heart…
Live in the question.

(Rainer Maria Rilke)

Simply spend 5 minutes a day in quiet. Do this as faithfully as possible. Find a time and space that works for you. If you cannot achieve that start with one minute and increase it as you are able. If you cannot do that take a deep cleansing breath each time you think of it during the day.

The greatest spiritual secret to strength might be the ability to keep perspective in life. The Serenity Prayer might be the ultimate expression of that. Try sitting quietly and slowly repeat it once a day for a month and see if you experience increased ability to find inner peace.

The Serenity Prayer

God grant me the serenity
to accept the things I cannot change;
courage to change the things I can;
and wisdom to know the difference.

Living one day at a time;
Enjoying one moment at a time;
Accepting hardships as the pathway to peace;
Taking, as He did, this sinful world
as it is, not as I would have it;
Trusting that He will make all things right
if I surrender to His Will;
That I may be reasonably happy in this life
and supremely happy with Him
Forever in the next.
Amen.

--Reinhold Niebuhr

Conclusion

This is not the end; it is just the beginning...

How are you feeling? We hope you feel energized, excited, and hopeful to continue your journey with new insight and direction. It will be helpful to periodically take time to reread sections of the book and your reflection notes, talk with your spouse and your children about promises needing to be made and followed through on. We hope and pray that you will make the years ahead more rewarding, healthier, and more satisfying as you travel as a person, as a partner, and as a family.

We want to end this part of our journey together with you with an adaptation of a prayer and a meditation from John Powell, S.J.

There is an old Christian tradition that
God sends each person into the world
With a special message to deliver,
With a song to sing for others,
With a special act of love to bestow.
No one else can speak my message,
Or sing my song, or offer my act of love.
These have been entrusted only to me.

According to this tradition,
The message may be spoken, the song sung,
The act of love delivered
Only to a few or to all the people in a small town,
Or to all the people in a large city,
Or even to all the people in the whole world.
It all depends on God's unique plan
For each unique person.

So from our hearts we want to say this to you:
Please believe that
You have an important message to deliver,
You have a beautiful song to sing,
And a unique act of love
To warm this world and to brighten its darkness.

And when the final history of this work is written,
Your message, your song, and your love
Will be recorded gratefully and forever.
You are in our hearts and our prayers always.

Peace, Kathie and Doug

<u>*References*</u>

Bradshaw, J. (1990). *Homecoming: reclaiming your inner child. New York: Bantam Books.*

Chapman, G. (2010). The 5 love languages: the secret to love that lasts. Chicago: Northfield Publishing.

De Mellow, A. (1988). Taking flight: a book of story meditations. New York: Doubleday.

Dickenson, E. (1955). Complete poems of Emily Dickenson. Johnson, T. (Ed.). Boston: Little, Brown and Company.

Frankl, V. (1959). *Man's search for meaning.* Boston: Beacon Books.

Girzone, J. (1994). *Never alone.* New York: Random House.

Gleeson, C. (2003). A canopy of stars: reflections for the journey. Melbourne: David Lovell Publishing.

Harris, T. (1969). I'm OK- you're OK. New York: Harper Collins Publisher.

Keith, K. M. (2002). Anyway: the paradoxical commandments: finding personal meaning in a crazy world. New York: Putnam.

Oliver, M. (1992). New and selected poems. Boston: Beacon Press.

Peck, M. S. (1997). *The road less traveled.* New York: Touchstone.